TONY SOPRANO
ON
MANAGEMENT

TONY SOPRANO
—ON—
MANAGEMENT

LEADERSHIP LESSONS INSPIRED
BY AMERICA'S FAVORITE MOBSTER

Anthony Schneider

BERKLEY BOOKS, NEW YORK

A Berkley Book
Published by The Berkley Publishing Group
A division of Penguin Group (USA) Inc.
375 Hudson Street
New York, New York 10014

TONY SOPRANO ON MANAGEMENT

This is an original publication of The Berkley Publishing Group.

Copyright 2004 by Anthony Schneider
Book design by Tiffany Estreicher
Cover design by Jill Boltin
Cover photograph by Antonio Mo/Taxi

First Edition: February 2004
Berkley trade paperback ISBN: 0-425-19494-9

This book has been catalogued with the Library of Congress.

Printed in the United States of America

10 9 8 7 6 5 4 3 2

For June and David

What do we mean when we say leadership?

—Tony Soprano

CONTENTS

THE TONY SOPRANO APPROACH

No More Fires

When the New Jersey crime family garbage war escalates, Tony Soprano swoops in. He summons the two feuding lieutenants to a standup meeting, hears them out, gets the facts, then tells them both, "All right, fix it. No more fires." He's in, he's out. He identifies the problem, figures out a solution, acts. Estimated time: about three and a half minutes. Welcome to the Tony Soprano approach.

Mob Boss CEO

Tony Soprano has never read a management book. He doesn't know about performance reviews or knowledge management, hasn't studied negotiation tactics. Yet he spends much of his time successfully managing a diverse workforce in a treacherous—and potentially deadly— business environment.

In an age of economic uncertainty, corporate turmoil, anxiety and downsizing, leaders are being forced to work at warp speed with different methods, new systems and shifting teams. Mergers force sweeping changes upon organizations, and increased competition adds pressures and problems, while downsizing, outsourcing and new technologies cause workers to take on new responsibilities. Our jobs—and the fabric of American business—have changed dramatically over the past decade, leaving the management mantras of yesterday behind, piles of books gathering dust. Businesses are moving faster, and jobs, companies, products and services are changing more rapidly than ever before. Meanwhile employees and consumers alike are wary of corporations and their leaders.

Managers complain that they don't have the time or resources to manage effectively. Business leaders say they are trapped by economic uncertainty, hostile boards, financial markets or stockholder demands to improve short-term results. At the same time, some recent managerial trends, such as hive-like corporate structures and flattened organizations with no job titles or set responsibilities, are going the way of eight-track tapes and Chia Pets.

Leaders must step up and steer new courses to get their companies back on track and regain public confidence. They must adapt to meet the challenges of today's business environments. And Tony Soprano is the surprising role model for this new breed of leader. His methods may appear unconventional, but we can all learn strategies and tactics from the way that he manages people, resolves conflict, negotiates and leads.

Not Since Attila the Hun

By any measure, Tony is a born leader. He has confidence and charisma, brains and empathy, inspires loyalty and reverence, and his power is rarely questioned. As "Paulie Walnuts" Gualtieri explains to a stubborn wiseguy: "The Boss of the Family told you you're gonna be Santa Claus. You're Santa Claus." The elements of the natural leader that Tony possesses in spades are characteristics that good leaders have shared since time immemorial. He is strong and courageous, confident and credible. He possesses a combination of unflinching strategic vision and the ability to get things done.

Granted, Tony is an unlikely candidate for the pages of *Fortune* magazine or the *Harvard Business Review*. He's the boss of a crime family, after all. But at his best he's a master at a new kind of management style. It's unorthodox. In fact, it often flies in the face of traditional management wisdom. Tony doesn't believe in democratic organizations and consensus building. He believes in authority. He delegates and allows autonomy, but he exerts pressure. He's not open to all suggestions all the time. When Ralph Cifaretto voices an objection to a decision made by another captain, Tony cuts him off: "Anybody ask for your input?" The Tony Soprano approach stresses structure, hierarchy and values. There are no metrics or paradigms, no management goals or rubrics, only results. He doesn't go in for peer reviews or stock options, just a slap on the back at the Bada Bing and an envelope full of cash. And it works. His team is cohesive, his business successful. By any measure, he is an effective leader.

The Tony Soprano Approach

As a leader, Tony is constantly dealing with new people and new problems. He leads during times of perpetual change and shifting adversity, with a lot of stress and few allies. He manages effectively despite insufficient resources and too little time. Sound familiar? The Tony Soprano approach is new and different. But if it weren't, and if it didn't work, no one would need this book.

Warp Speed

The Tony Soprano approach is fast, aiming to create and save an essential business commodity—time. In the five minutes it takes to sip an espresso, Tony analyzes a situation, listens to the background and arrives at a decision. Bada boom.

Today's leaders must work at warp speed, adapt to new conditions and manage change. Being good isn't enough. You have to be swift and nimble as well. Tony Soprano manages fast, and that's one of the reasons he's able to manage so many different personalities involved in so many areas of nefarious business. He doesn't waste time; business matters are dealt with carefully and judiciously, but always quickly. He doesn't work longer hours. Instead, he works more efficiently and makes decisions faster.

It's Okay to Squeeze

Tony takes a hands-on, proactive approach to leadership. He expects the best, he is demanding, and he knows how to use muscle to get what he wants. Tony fosters autonomy, yet he also knows how to squeeze to get results. It's called constructive manipulation, and it's not a bad thing. Not anymore.

Tony is not a bully on a power trip. He squeezes silently, or at least quietly, and he exerts pressure in the service of a project or decision, not because he feels like bossing people around. Nor does he rely on rank or his ability to intimidate. Tony will cajole, persuade or manipulate to get the job done. Depending on whom he is managing, Tony adopts whatever is the most effective way of achieving his goals. He's an avuncular pal to Christopher Moltisanti, nudging, encouraging, egging him on to self-actualization and murder. He's a tough guy to the intractable Richie Aprile, laying down the law, pulling rank. And when people screw up? Fuggedaboudit. Tony busts balls. He doesn't wait; he does it now.

And good leaders don't only squeeze people. They squeeze everything. Business plans and ad campaigns, ideas and strategies, lunch breaks or holidays—good leaders push and question until they are the best they can be.

Decisiveness

Tony makes decisions fast, and they're usually the right decisions. And he sticks to his decisions. Whether he's deciding how to resolve internecine rivalries or what to do when his daughter's boyfriend appears in a strip club carrying a piece, Tony makes the best, fastest decision he can based on the information available.

"A wrong decision is better than indecision," Tony is fond of saying. Decisiveness helps him to be a more efficient leader, a better negotiator and a faster implementer. It buys one thing that money cannot: time.

Direct and Transparent

Uncle T favors directness, with a focus on candor not consensus building. He has a keen sense of right and wrong, and sees things in black and white. He listens to his team, encourages them to get involved in discussions and decisions, but at the end of the day, it's his way or the highway.

Tony doesn't beat around the bush, whether dealing with subordinates, business partners or anyone else. When Uncle Junior pushes too hard, Tony shoots him down: "Hey, I'm on the street," he says. "That's the arrangement." He is a transparent leader, open about his feelings and goals. When profit margins dip, he calls an executive meeting, discloses financials, then lets them have it.

Personal and Personalized

The Tony Soprano approach is intensely personal, with a focus on people, not systems. He understands that people are an organization's most important asset, and he prioritizes personal relationships as the building blocks of successful teams and organizations. He gets inside people's heads. He figures them out, and uses that knowledge to communicate better and lead more effectively.

The personal nature of the Tony Soprano approach means that relationships grow faster and deeper, and each person is treated as an individual. Tony assesses each captain, and he delegates and organizes according to the talents, inclinations and skills of each individual. Finding the right role for each employee creates teams that are efficient and function smoothly.

Organized and Calm

Being fast isn't enough. Tony knows that effective leaders must be organized and calm. Well, most of the time. Watch Tony when a dead body
surfaces, or when there's the threat of an informer, even when he's on
a business call and his mother phones to say there's a fire in her house.
He keeps his cool, goes through a series of steps to deal with the problem and comes up with a plan. He may not always look it on the outside, but he is calm and organized, even when the world around him is
exploding.

Trust and Loyalty

Lying means death, literally, on *The Sopranos*, metaphorically in relationships and on Wall Street. Even crooked cops trust Tony, because "At
least with Tony Soprano, you know where you stand." Tony is tough.
Cross him at your own peril. But he won't trick you, and he won't betray your trust. And it is his transparency and trustworthiness, rather
than his power or bullying, that make him a leader worth following.

You can only succeed as a leader with the backing of a loyal team.
That's why effective leaders deserve and insist upon loyalty. They are
loyal to their team, and their team is loyal to them and to each other. In
an industry where alliances can turn on a dime and the diminution of
loyalty gets someone a bullet in the chest, Tony is surrounded by a re-
markably loyal team. He knows he must earn respect and trust, knows
he must understand the dreams and desires of each member of his team
to maintain their loyalty—and survive.

Delegation

Tony is a master at delegating. That's why he's able to maintain so many businesses and business relationships. He tells one of his *capos:* "It's your job to make my job easier."

Tony delegates tasks that are not time-effective for him and functions that allow others to grow and succeed. He rarely gets involved with the day-to-day operations of the many businesses he owns or controls. Rather, he manages captains and partners who, in turn, run the various subsidiaries. The idea is simple: teach your team to fish. Empower and train your team, and you effectively establish lasting systems and processes, while charting a clear course for career advancement.

Hierarchy

Tony hankers for the bygone era when rank meant everything, authority was respected, the family was a sacred institution, and rules were never broken. "We follow codes," he explains to Dr. Melfi, and lists the pillars of his value system: "honor and family and loyalty."

Tony's leadership style is old school—well, new old school. He likes structure, rules and hierarchy, especially when he's sitting on top. He doesn't pretend that every team member has an equal say, although he is willing to listen. He doesn't see the organization as horizontal, hive-like or anything other than a ladder from least to most powerful. He manages from the top down and believes that people must learn by doing—and climb the company ladder one rung at a time.

Flexibility

Even though Tony espouses structure and hierarchy, he remains flexible. Just as flexible manufacturing creates better products and increases speed to market, flexible leadership results in stronger, swifter teams.

Tony rolls with the punches. He responds and adapts. Job descriptions change overnight. He moves people in and out of leadership roles, hires, promotes and fires in order to get the best fit and make sure his team shares his vision. And he expects those around him to be just as flexible, as new alliances are formed and old associates are killed or go to jail.

Execution

Tony knows how to execute. (And we're not talking about clipping people.) He produces the results he promises; he makes good on his vision. He doesn't sit around and think about getting things done. He acts. People trust him because they know he will deliver the goods, and that's why he's a good guy to go into business with. Like other effective leaders, Tony doesn't work hard, he works well; doesn't get lots of things done, but gets the right things done. And Tony expects his team and partners to be equally effective, to deliver what they promise on time and on budget.

Executing well means being a captain of change, and Tony spends a lot of time transforming the company he leads. He adopts new methods and processes, enters new markets, shuts down unprofitable arms. For example, he redefines Uncle Junior's role, renegotiates his percentage of revenues and redistributes his power.

Ability and Desire

Finally, Tony leads well because he wants to lead. "I am the mother-fuckin' fuckin' one who calls the shots" is how he puts it. He has a clear vision, a smart strategy and a plan for how to get there. He wants his business to succeed and each member of his team to excel. He hires well, delegates well, communicates effectively and trains his team to the best of his abilities. He inspires confidence, builds energy and enthusiasm and sets the standards that every employee must uphold. Sure, Uncle T doesn't always get it right. His final attempt at constructive manipulation with Ralph Cifaretto ends not in communication and team building, but with body parts in a bathtub. Still, at his best, Tony aspires to a new brand of leadership and personifies a dynamic management paradigm that is as effective as it is timely.

How to Use This Book, or You Can't Just Whack 'Em

This book is designed for leaders and managers, people at the top or on their way there. Whether you work in a large business or a small one, the public sector or not-for-profit world, the Tony Soprano approach can help you lead better and work more efficiently, effectively and happily.

If you're looking for a guide to running a syndicated crime family, however, this book may not be right for you. For most of us, having a cup of coffee with a business partner means exactly that: going to a nearby Starbucks and talking shop over a latte, as opposed to Tony's definition of having coffee with a business acquaintance. What he really means is that he chased a man onto the sidewalk and beat the bejeezus out of him. The rest of us don't get to do that when someone pisses us off. Violence is not an acceptable response to workplace conflict. Nor do we get to take disloyal subordinates on a one-way boat ride. We don't clip people who quit, or go over to a subordinate's house to beat them up, no matter what they did. Even if your coworker talks to a competitor, killing the guy is not an accepted or judicious response. You can't just whack 'em.

So, *Tony Soprano on Management* focuses on strategies, tools and tactics that have a more universal appeal and won't result in unexplained deaths or prison sentences. The book incorporates strategies for leadership with specific tactics for managers, using examples from *The Sopranos* and the real world. Direct and easy-to-use, each chapter includes helpful pointers, worksheets, call-outs and rules, as well as case studies and wrap-ups to summarize key points.

ONE

KNOW THYSELF

Hello, Doctor Melfi

When we first meet Tony Soprano, he's in a therapist's office. Specifically, he's in the waiting room of Dr. Jennifer Melfi's office. Now, you may think that's no big deal, but for the "godfather of New Jersey," going to see a therapist is a huge deal. And what is more symbolic of a man on a quest of self-knowledge than standing in the waiting room before his first meeting with a therapist?

Tony realizes (albeit kicking and screaming) that it's a good place to be and that knowing more about himself might be the key to his sanity, happiness and success. Knowing yourself and understanding your tendencies as a person and leader are keys to becoming a better person and a more effective leader. Not that it's easy work. Self-knowledge, insight and psychiatry don't come easy. Certainly not to Tony. "Apparently what you're feeling is not what you're feeling," he complains, "and what you're not feeling is your real agenda."

Who Am I? Where Am I Going?

Tony Soprano has realized rather late in life that until you really know yourself, know your strengths, weaknesses, dreams, goals and fears, you cannot achieve real success or happiness. That's why he's in Dr. Melfi's office. He knows himself well enough to know he's lacking in the self-knowledge department, and he has the candor, intelligence and resources (including a good therapist) to get there. Tony is very good at his job. He's less good at his life, and he knows that until he figures out why, he won't be the best person or the best leader he can be.

Knowing yourself means self-examination. Dr. Melfi instructs Tony: "We'll have to delve deeper, focus." Knowing yourself also means liking yourself and taking time for yourself.

Knowing yourself means hard work, addressing weaknesses, figuring out your psyche, being true to yourself. It means having and showing integrity, separating who you are from who you want to be, and charting a course to reach the person and place you want to be.

When Tony takes Meadow to Bowdoin College, he sees a plaque with a quote by Hawthorne: "No man can wear one face to himself and another to the multitude without finally getting bewildered as to which may be true." Tony's panic attacks are brutal proof that he cannot hide the truth from himself.

Goals Are Good

In self-knowledge and personal growth, just as in other spheres of life and work, it is useful to set goals and measure your progress. Dr. Melfi asks Tony to keep a log, to record his feelings of anxiety and anger as well as memories of panic attacks. First, get the facts, then figure out what they mean.

Fears, Foibles and Fairness

Even the best leaders have fears, foibles or prejudices. That's okay. What's important is to know yourself well enough that you know your own tendencies so they don't get in the way, and recognize your biases so they don't cloud your judgment.

Tony Soprano is quick to anger. He knows that. Half the time, when people piss him off, he slugs or threatens them. But he knows this isn't the best response to news he doesn't want to hear or an opinion he doesn't share, and he's working hard to control his anger. He realizes that in order to be more successful as a leader, husband and father, he needs a calmer disposition—think first, punch second.

Tony is also a racist. He doesn't want Meadow hanging out with Noah, an African-American Columbia University undergraduate. Tony knows his prejudices get in his way, and he's better at undoing them in the business arena than he is at home. When he deals with Reverend James, an African-American civil activist, Tony shows respect and mutual understanding.

Just about every manager has her pet peeve, her hot button. Most of them are perfectly valid complaints like tardiness or sloppy work. And they're right: people should be on time; all work should be neat and well presented. But it's important to remember that, for the most part, people don't intend to screw up. Just about every manager also has her problem child, the bad apple who seems to do more wrong than anyone else. And it is possible that he or she is more apt to mess up. Even so, you

---

▪ WORKSHEET ▪
Self-Knowledge Pop Quiz

....

What are your hot buttons? What issues are you bringing to the office with you that need to be resolved in order for you to work more effectively? In many cases, anger, guilt or sadness are clues to the psyche.

When do you lose your temper? What causes it to happen at home? At work?

_____

_____

Think of things that happened recently that ticked you off. Is there a pattern?

_____

_____

Which colleague, client, family member makes you angry the most often? Why?

_____

_____

When your spouse, sibling, partner says something about work that ticks you off, why is it making you angry? What is the truth behind what they're saying?

_____

_____

Are there days when you walk into the office already angry? Why?

_____

_____

What happens at the office that makes you sad? What fear or memory is behind that feeling?

_____

_____

Do you sometimes feel guilty? Why?

_____

_____

How can you predict what will make you sad, guilty, angry? How could it be avoided or controlled?

_____

_____

What are your self-knowledge goals? How are you working toward them?

_____

_____

Keep a log of psychological issues or problems.

_____

_____

can't mete out different punishments based on who screws up or your personal misdemeanor ranking. It's important to be fair, and vital that you not prejudge, that you listen to what is being said, not who is saying it, that you respond to an action, not who did it. Leaders effectively speak for the company, stockholders or senior management, so they must be objective not personal.

Fairness is essential to any good relationship. It's especially important that bosses act fairly toward all and are perceived as fair and impartial. Consistency ensures that everyone has a good sense of people and, especially, their leaders. When Tony's sister, Janice, steals the prosthetic leg of their mother's Russian nurse, Tony doesn't side with or protect his sister. He is equally tough and imposes the same rules of justice and ethics on everyone. In his case these rules are hard and unforgiving. He likes and trusts Paulie, but snaps at him when he suggests a course of action that violates the code of conduct. Tony is tough but consistent, and his top team knows it.

Case Study

Rodney, a Londoner, runs a magazine in New York and has strong opinions about dress code and demeanor. He thinks short-sleeve shirts should only be worn out of the office, believes that jackets should be worn to all meetings, and judges people by their shoes and shirts. After a while, he realizes that New Yorkers have a more casual dress code than Londoners. He comes to understand that his judgments have more to do with British standards and norms than American propriety or business etiquette. He may not always like the way his staff dresses, but he knows better than to judge them for it. With his vision unclouded by sartorial differences, he is able to apply himself to managing people without judging them based on personal standards. Businesspeople, like everyone else, must assess and dismantle prejudices, or they will get in the way of good relationships and good business.

BE FAIR AND CONSISTENT

Are you fair and consistent? Whether praising or punishing, ask yourself:

➤ Do you treat people equally?

➤ Do you tend to get mad at the same people all the time? Do they really screw up all the time?

➤ Do you get angry based on your personal code of rules and morals, or based on the severity of the screwup?

➤ Are you being objective or personal?

Got to Admit It's Getting Better

The path toward self-knowledge is long and difficult. Tony struggles to learn about himself, and struggles to change when he does gain insight into himself. Just because you want to know yourself doesn't mean it's easy to get there. As Tony demonstrates, self-knowledge is hard to come by, but it is vital to personal growth and leadership development.

As leadership guru Warren Bennis puts it: "You make your life your own by understanding it."[1] And we have tools and resources to help us on that path. Bennis calls these the four lessons of self-knowledge:

One: You are your own best teacher.

Two: Accept responsibility. Blame no one.

Three: You can learn anything you want to learn.

Four: True understanding comes from reflecting on your experience.[2]

Hey, if Tony Soprano can do it, so can you.

The better you know yourself the better leader you become. You won't get tripped up by knee-jerk emotional responses, won't be inconsistent or unfair, won't let yourself be blinded by anger or prejudices. Knowing yourself also means that you are able to understand and empathize with others. You become a better judge of others' character when you have a firm footing with your own. Tony is a shrewd judge of character, thanks in part to attaining self-knowledge and being observant. At a business dinner with an allied family in Naples, he comments on the behavior of the leader apparent of the Italian family: "Nino, he's insecure," Tony says. "It affects everything he says."

KNOW YOURSELF

Are you taking steps towards self-knowledge as a person, colleague, boss?

➤ Know your fears, what makes you angry or sad.

➤ Understand what personal issues get in the way of your work.

➤ Take responsibility for your behavior.

➤ Know yourself better today than you did yesterday.

The Symptoms: Honesty and Integrity

The symptoms of self-knowledge are honesty and integrity. And just about all employees agree that these are two of the most important things a leader can give them.

Honesty and integrity are vital when dealing with both work and home families. When Tony drives Meadow to New England to look at colleges, his honesty is tested when Meadow asks if he is in the Mafia. He denies it initially, then comes clean and admits that some of his income is derived from illegitimate sources. Meadow is thrilled that her dad is being honest with her, and it's a bonding moment: Tony and Meadow tell each other, probably for the first time in a long time, that they love each other.

Who Moved My Sense of Humor?

Knowing yourself means understanding yourself and not taking yourself too seriously. Work is often stressful, difficult and tiring, and that's when we look to our leaders for support and strength. So it is crucial that they be dependable, have integrity and optimism. You can't be in a bad mood—well, not unless there's a good reason. You can't have an off day. Leaders set the example, every day, in every way. They are on stage all the time, and everything they do is closely watched, analyzed and interpreted by those around them. Hewlett-Packard CEO Carly Fiorina puts it this way: "Leadership is a performance. You have to be conscious about your behavior, because everyone else is."

It's important to smile. If you're smiling, then surely things are going well, you're winning, open to suggestions, happy. And isn't that what we all want in our bosses and coworkers? Maintaining a sense of humor makes you a more fun person to work with and tells others that you're approachable, open to new ideas. Having a sense of humor shows that you don't take yourself too darn seriously, that you're congenial and receptive to ideas. And receptiveness and openness are vital to becoming a better team leader, a better coach and enabler.

A lot of leaders just don't feel up to it every day. They complain that it's a charade to pretend to be calm and happy when they're going nuts over the weekly management meeting or poor sales figures. But good leaders do it anyway. "You have to bring your game face every day," says Oxygen Media COO Lisa Hall. Everyone is watching, so the leader sets the tone. And we all know that levity is contagious. Act like you're in a good mood, and you never know, you might just be in a good mood soon, and others may follow suit.

Tony may be tough, and he definitely has a short fuse, but he's dependable and he has a great sense of humor that rarely deserts him. Even when he's stressed out or yelling at someone, Tony maintains his humor.

Yeah, and Your Company Too

Even as Tony is getting to know himself, he's busy in another realm of self-knowledge. He's working with *capos* and soldiers (not to mention allied bosses) to make sure the business knows itself. Especially when strategies, markets and partners change so fast, as they do for the Soprano family business, it is vital that the employees know the business. That's why Tony spends a lot of time explaining strategy and sharing his vision of the future. Tony understands that it's important that he know the organization and that the organization knows itself. Many leaders call special meetings, or use meeting time, to disseminate organizational information. This is especially useful when there are major changes or rumors of changes—mergers, downsizing, new clients, acquisitions. It's important to remember that people may not know as much as you do, and they want to know—and deserve to know—about the team they're playing on.

It is important to have meetings about the business, strategy and ideas, not just today's client or tomorrow's product launch. And it is the job of the leader to foster team thinking, group communication, idea sharing and organizational self-knowledge.

THE WRAP-UP

If you asked Tony about Dr. Melfi, he'd probably beat you up and threaten your life if you let on that he was seeing a shrink. But let's say you got him talking about self-knowledge, here are a few pointers he might give you:

■ **WORKSHEET** ■
Leadership Preparedness

We all have some of the characteristics of a good leader. We all need to work to be better leaders. What are your strengths and weaknesses as a leader?

What abilities and characteristics make you a good leader?

_____

_____

_____

_____

What abilities and characteristics are you lacking?

_____

_____

_____

_____

Are you a good listener? How could you improve?

_____

_____

_____

_____

Who are your mentors? What mentoring relationships have you enabled?

_____

_____

_____

_____

Do you know everyone on your team personally? Have you spent one-on-one time with them out of the office, or not discussing work?

_____
_____
_____
_____

Who is loyal and why?

_____
_____
_____
_____

Who are the discontents and why?

_____
_____
_____
_____

How are you working to make sure your company knows itself and shares ideas?

_____
_____
_____
_____

- Self-knowledge is vital to good leadership. Some facets of self-knowledge are easier to master than others, but you keep trying anyway.

- Integrity has its own rewards.

- Ask important questions; chip away at big issues.

- A good therapist helps. A good family helps. Good friends help.

- Be fair and consistent dealing with others. Use objective, not personal, measures of performance.

- Be honest with yourself and others.

- Smile. Maintain your sense of humor.

- Make sure the players know about the team. Make sure the organization knows itself.

TWO

VISION IS LIKE GOOD BRACIOLE

The Vision Thing

Self-knowledge leads to vision. As you gain individual and organizational self-knowledge, you become able to see and attain your vision. Tony Soprano uses the personal insights he's gained to build and refine a vision for himself, his business and his family.

Bad leaders say they don't have time for vision. They have too much to do without worrying about artsy-fartsy ideas that don't contribute to the bottom line. Good leaders say vision is vital, and they spend a lot of time articulating, refining and communicating it.

What is vision exactly? Vision is a combination of goals, dreams, ideas and predictions. It is a destination—where you want to go—and a plan—how to get there. A good leader has a vision of his business, the future of the business, as well as how to run that business. A good leader has a vision of his life outside of work and of the lives of his team members and how they can be improved or made more secure, happy or meaningful. Vision statements usually begin with open-ended phrases like "It would be cool if . . ." or "We are working toward . . ."

Vision has at least two components—business and family, work and home. The work vision is a strategic overview based on a realistic knowledge of an organization's strengths and weaknesses, competitive advantages and the environment in which it operates. Family vision is a collaborative view shared with a spouse or partner that encompasses goals for lifestyle, children, home and education.

Tony has clear ideas about what he wants to do professionally and personally, and these ideas keep him on track even when he faces setbacks. As one made-man puts it, "Tony sees the big picture." Tony develops and refines his work vision by assessing the past, analyzing the landscape and consulting experts. He has examined the successes and failures of his father and the older generation of mobsters. He analyzes his competitors, assesses competitive advantages and market trends and receives counsel from a range of experts and people with common interests, including his team, business partners, his wife, lawyers and a psychiatrist.

A large part of Tony's work is about keeping the business on track, staying focused on more profitable ventures and areas that are, if not legit, then less illegal. As Christopher tells Adriana, focus is paramount: "Eyes on the prize." Tony wants to stay away from drugs and wars, and he pushes his *capos* to focus on business, not social issues and grievances. His family vision is equally important. Tony wants prosperity, happiness and security for Carmela, A.J. and Meadow.

Vision is not something you figure out and then you're done with it. Vision should be growing, changing and evolving. You must have an open mind, must seek the ideas, questions and objections of others in order to have a vision that is useful, informed and smart.

Know It

Superior leadership is built on superior vision. Good leaders take time to think about their vision—for themselves, their companies or groups, their coworkers, even their families. Wake up Tony in the middle of the night and ask him how, say, the Bada Bing club fits into his overall business strategy, and if he doesn't shoot you or throw you out of his bedroom, he'll tell you. You may not see him sitting around thinking about long-term goals and how to achieve them, but he does it. He knows where he wants to go, and he's always planning how to get there.

Good leaders, then, have a clear vision of their companies and themselves, their strengths and weaknesses as businesses, teams and leaders, and a strong sense of which areas could use some improvement.

Tony has a sense of the future, understands the market and has predicted opportunities and pitfalls for his business. He has an implacable knowledge of where he wants his business to go. For example, he likes stock market scams and investing in the Newark esplanade. He doesn't like drugs or roadside heists.

Tony is constantly researching market trends, always keeping an eye on relevant legal and financial issues. He teaches his team about RICO (Racketeer Influenced and Corrupt Organizations Act) and explicates the rules of entrapment. That's because he is planning for the future of the business, even while managing the present. New research and information inform a new vision, which in turn, allows a new strategy to be developed and implemented.

Grow It

Vision is free. You can't buy it, you don't read it, and you can't borrow it. You pretty much just sit there and think and try to see the future and figure out what's important, or smart, or lacking.

It's important to articulate your vision for self, work, home, family, industry, economy. All of it. The whole manicotti. As Yogi Berra said, "Predicting is difficult, especially the future." But it's important work. So get started. Or, if you've already started, keep at it.

To get there, it is necessary to see the forest, not just the trees. Successful leaders agree that time away from the office is vital for two reasons. First, it allows the office to run without the boss, which is crucial. Second, it gives the leader time away from the day-to-day tactical elements, which is necessary to think, see the big picture and plan. Holidays, long weekends, even a cup of coffee or a walk around the block can be rejuvenating, relieve stress and provide clarity. And energy and clarity are vital ingredients for cooking up a nourishing vision.

You improve your vision by broadening your knowledge, by reading books and industry reports, taking classes, talking to people in different departments, companies, industries. Tony talks to his psychiatrist, his top team, union leaders, a lawyer, even Herman "Hesh" Rabkin, a mob elder statesman. He puts it all together and comes up with his a vision for life, business and family.

SEEK ADVICE FROM EXPERTS

Tony goes to a psychiatrist because he is having panic attacks. He talks to Hesh about business, his family life, even his moodiness and panic attacks. Learn from the best:

➤ Seek out and listen to expert opinion.

➤ Make sure you have mentors.

➤ Find people in related positions in other organizations who are good teachers and role models.

➤ Read about effective leaders and successful companies in other industries.

➤ Befriend elder statesmen and people whom you admire. Listen to them.

Tony knows that teaching is as important as learning. And he tries to impart his knowledge and vision to others. He brings Bobby "Bacala" Baccalieri up to speed after his promotion and spends a lot of time mentoring Christopher, grooming him to be a leader. When someone is promoted, or when a capable lieutenant rises through the ranks of an organization, the effective leader gets involved, taking the time to get together, listen and educate.

The Sopranos serves up a taste of the other kind of leader as well. Uncle Junior lacks vision, listens to uncorroborated rumors, and takes advice from idiotic captains and vituperative widows. He doesn't do research, nor does he listen to consultants or seek expert opinion. And the result? Junior's end of the business goes south.

Vision Means Focus and Boundaries

Having a cohesive professional and personal vision means focusing on the right areas—the things you'd like to improve; changes you believe will bring about profits, improved products or higher employee satisfaction. Look at Tony: he's dealing with his panic attacks, working toward better profit margins and moving into more lucrative business endeavors. He keeps the business focused on business, not personal vendettas or factional wars. The only reason Tony's crew does not go to war with Uncle Junior's boys is Tony. He navigates a peaceful solution to a seemingly insoluble problem.

Tony may not write down his vision and revise it continually; but if he did have that file in his office or document on his laptop, it would contain words like focus, family, innovation, security, profitability.

Vision Means Innovation

Tony's vision for the future of his business is different from anything his father knew or imagined—more agile, more legal and more profitable. Tony is moving the company away from some of the traditional niches, such as the protection racket and loan-sharking, into new areas with better opportunities for profit and competitive advantage, like real estate and stocks. Okay, make that low-income housing scams and brokerage fraud. So they ain't exactly legal, but they are smart, strategic plays. Tony is expanding into areas where his business can achieve and sustain competitive advantage and enjoy higher earnings and better profit margins. He is one of the most successful people in his industry, and that's because of his ability to innovate, to find new businesses, partners and markets. He encourages creativity, listens to new ways of doing things, is open to new business ideas.

The successful leader is always open to change and innovation. She ensures that channels of communication are open, and she listens to new ideas. She takes action to encourage innovation. Good leaders ask team members to share ideas and think about how things could be done better, differently, more effectively. Many companies reserve part of their intranet for posting and shaping innovative products, services or approaches.

And Uncle Junior? Bearer of the flag of the un–Tony Soprano approach. You get the feeling the last innovation he cared about was the remote control. All he can think about is waste management, card games and grocery coupons. And whose business is better? Whose house is bigger? Who has more toys?

Vision means shaking things up, forgetting worn-out ideas, destroying yesterday's machines. To paraphrase business guru Tom Peters, innovation means embracing the new and erasing the old. "Innovation = eraser mania"[1] is how Peters puts it, and he warns of "the perils of polishing yesterday's apple."[2] Even good vision must be reinvented and reinvigorated. And effective leaders make their vision better by surrounding themselves with smart people and listening to their ideas.

INNOVATE NOW

Tony is taking his business into new areas and getting rid of old people, processes and ideas. Encourage innovation:

➤ Think big.

➤ Encourage creativity.

➤ Think differently, laterally.

➤ Destroy old ideas.

➤ Ask for new ideas and listen to them.

➤ Get out of areas of business that are washed up, dangerous or unprofitable.

➤ Look for new markets, clients, partners, demographics.

Sallie Krawcheck, CEO of Smith Barney, has been making headlines because of the ways she is changing the direction and structure of her company as a result of her vision of the financial services sector and the future of retail brokerage in America. She's got the vision thing. Tony would probably like her. Carmela definitely would.

▪ WORKSHEET ▪
See the Future

Ask questions to arrive at a workable vision. Ask yourself, ask your spouse or partner, friends, coworkers and business associates. The answers are not, in themselves, your vision, but they will help you get there.

What is your vision for your group, company, organization?

_____

_____

_____

Complete this sentence: It would be cool if . . .

_____

_____

_____

Complete this sentence: We are working toward . . .

_____

_____

_____

Complete this sentence: I lead best when I . . .

_____

_____

_____

Complete this sentence: I am a less effective leader when I . . .

_____

_____

_____

Complete this sentence: We need to focus on . . .

_____

_____

_____

What problems do you need to solve? At work? At home?

_____

_____

_____

Think about your best competitor, or a company in a related space that you admire. What three things do they do well? What can you learn from them?

_____

_____

_____

Complete this sentence: Three big changes that will impact our company or industry are . . .

_____

_____

_____

How are you changing and innovating? What are you erasing? What are you creating?

_____

_____

_____

How can your company or group benefit from the changes you see impacting your company or industry? How will you need to adapt in order to benefit?

_____

_____

_____

How will your company or organization be different in one year? Three years? Five years?

_____

_____

_____

How will you be different? Smarter? Better?

_____

_____

_____

Vision Is Personal Too

Vision must be personal and personalized, extending beyond a leader's vision of his self to encompass team, coworkers or group. Tony has a clear vision for his top team, knows who they are and where they will be in three or five years. He has plans for Sil, Paulie and Christopher, has a vision for what they need to learn, what parts of the business they need to become familiar with. It's about growth. Also, he has a vision for the bad apples, like Ralph and Richie. It's about containment.

Ideally, a leader's vision should be informed by the vision of co-workers both above and below her. The cycle of vision, constantly fueling and being fueled by input from others, ensures both creativity and consistency of vision. The best leader, then, is not a dictator but the hub of an executive team, not an oracle but an enabler of vision.

The difference between business and team vision is not whether you have it—good leaders have both—but how and when you communicate it. Tony shares his vision for the company and its business units, but he keeps his feelings about people like Ralph and Richie pretty much to himself. He doesn't like them, but Ralph is a good earner and Richie is the brother of the former boss. So Uncle T keeps his complaints to himself, limits exposure, gives them the opportunity to prove themselves. When they don't, when they screw up, he is prepared for that, and he is not afraid to ruffle feathers, to criticize them and shake things up for the good of the company.

Colin Powell stresses the idea that good leaders inevitably piss some people off. "By trying not to get anyone mad, and by treating everyone equally 'nicely,'" Powell says, "the only people you'll wind up angering are the most creative and productive people in the organization."[3]

Of course, good leaders don't expect failure and shouldn't coddle creative types or clip the problem child. But they should have a vision of how each team member will add to the group as a whole, a strategy for each person's growth, development and contribution.

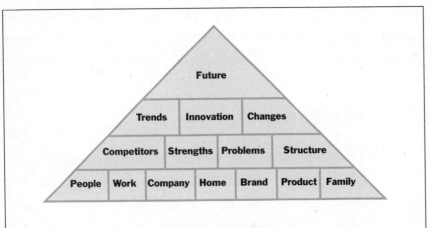

THE VISION PYRAMID

From CEO to vice president to regional manager and so on, everyone needs a vision pyramid. Each pyramid derives ideas and consistency from the one below it, and each pyramid also sends ideas upward to the pyramid above it.

Squeeze the Vision

It's okay to squeeze, to put your vision through the wringer. Question it, poke holes in it, rethink, rework. For example, if you've identified an area of competitive advantage, ask yourself what it really means and why you have it. If you have made assumptions about the future, question them. Challenge your predictions, reexamine your innovations, think through worst-case scenarios, kick the strategic tires.

When Darwin Smith took the helm of Kimberly-Clark, the once mighty paper company's stock had fallen and sales were flat. Smith transformed the company. He had a vision and he made good on it: he sold paper mills and focused instead on building consumer brands.[4]

During the twenty years that he was CEO, annual sales increased seven-fold, and today Kleenex and other Kimberly-Clark brands are among the best-known consumer products in over 150 countries.[5]

Case Study

Clara, CEO of a consumer food company, is saddled with navigating her company and its brands through a recession. She starts with a vision, a focus on going back to basics, on core competencies, on pushing for growth of major product lines rather than looking for the next big thing. Given the past strategies of former CEOs interested in everything from e-commerce opportunities to sports nutrition bars and other research-intensive products, Clara's vision is nothing short of a revolution for the company.

Clara turns her vision into a business strategy supporting specific tactics and goals, and she shares that vision. The marketing group reshuffles budgets, increases ad spending on the core brands and squeezes budgets of the less profitable products and untested gambles. Research and production move toward a more streamlined organization, outsourcing anything that is not a core function. Clara changes gears on acquisitions, looking to buy proven products already out of the gate, rather than always developing new ones in-house. She builds up management teams around the top brands and essential projects. She extends the top brands via new products, aiming at new markets and demographics.

Clara's goals are increased market share and profits, not media attention or new products. She makes projections, defines ways to judge whether and how much the core brands perform better, measures profit margins and market share. Over time she reassesses and revises her vision and the paths to get there.

We Ain't the Church

Tony works hard to steer the business toward more profitable areas of enterprise and away from involvements that are more social in nature. He opposes doing things for strictly personal reasons, whether those reasons have to do with retribution or more noble instincts. That's why he rejects Silvio's plans to quash Native-American protests over Columbus Day. "We're running a business here," he tells Silvio. And while he often relents—Tony's crew does get involved in the Columbus Day protests after all—his vision is clear, and he lets people know when he's making an exception or doing them a favor.

Tony's vision for work and life serves as a rubric for judging different approaches and adjudicating debates, and allows him to reach quick decisions on any idea presented by a team member. If something is in line with his vision, then he does it; if it's not, he questions it.

Show It

Vision is no good in a vacuum. One of the most significant results of a leader having a good, well-articulated vision is that it provides a basis for cohesion and gives other people something to aim for. Tony knows that if his crew shares his business vision, then they are more likely to think and act like a unified team. He also knows that he can give everyone in his organization something to aspire to, some common goals that are part of a shared vision for the future. Tony inspires others by sharing his vision. When Paulie complains about day-to-day operations, Tony reminds him about the Newark esplanade project and how much money he will earn.

Communicate

A shared vision is a million times more valuable than silent vision. That's why many of Tony's business meetings with his *capos* are equal part tactics and vision. He keeps their eyes on the prize—winning construction contracts rather than stealing fiber-optic cable. And he builds trust, gathers feedback and instills a sense of unity by sharing his vision.

It is incumbent upon leaders to articulate and communicate their vision, to explain and discuss strategic goals to their teams, listen to feedback and review and revise both vision and strategy. Indeed, it is up to the leader to ensure that vision and values are shared and that teams and organizations are committed to common goals. Some CEOs hold town hall meetings to communicate vision and elicit feedback. Many team leaders hold "lunch and learn" meetings where someone presents the findings of a recent study, reports on a new book or trade show he attended. The idea is to get people to think in terms of market trends, big picture issues, vision and strategy. Whatever form they take, it's a good idea to hold meetings that are not about a particular client or project.

SHARE THE VISION

Take time to share your vision of your company or organization, and encourage others to grow and share their vision:

➤ Start with short-term goals.

➤ Move on to long-term goals: where are we going, how do we get there.

➤ Help people to stay current with trends affecting your industry, clients or competitors.

➤ Help people to think creatively about your industry, trends, technologies.

➤ Talk about strategies and long-term goals. Share your vision.

A shared vision becomes a basis for trust and a cornerstone of delegation. It's because Tony knows that Sil and Paulie share his vision for the company that he is able to say "Take care of it" and know that they will get it right, whatever the project is. Pfizer CEO Hank McKinnell has a simple response when people ask his advice on a particular project: "Understand the vision and values of the organization. Then you figure it out."[6]

Commit to the Vision

Tony has a vision for the success of his business, the sanctity of his home, the growth of his family, and he's working to make it happen.

The Newark esplanade, protection from the FBI, and Meadow and A.J. going to college—these are the stars he steers by. Maybe he'll achieve them and maybe he won't, but he's sure going to try. As Wal-Mart founder Sam Walton puts it: "Commit to your goals."

THE WRAP-UP

You gotta have vision. You don't see Tony noodling over the various aspects of his vision, but you get the sense that he thinks about it a lot. He has a vision of his business and where it's going, a plan for each and every *capo* and made-man, and he's working on refining and communicating the different aspects of his vision.

Vision is about the future not the present, strategy not tactics, the invisible not the tangible, questions not answers, problems not solutions, creativity not repetition, life not job:

- Vision is a map of the future and a plan for how to get there.

- Start today. Vision is iterative. The sooner you get started, the better it will become.

- Articulate your vision for work, growth, the future, employees, life.

- Take time out of your day to think about vision and long-term projects.

- Get out of the office. Try to see things from five thousand feet to predict trends and plan for the future.

- Refine your vision by seeking expert opinion from consultants, colleagues, your team and others.

- Innovate now. Make new products or services. Try new processes. Think laterally, outside the box, farther afield.

- Predict the future. Change your vision and make plans based on your predictions.

- Share the vision so that people can contribute and so that you communicate your plans for the future and how to get there.

- Put your vision through the wringer. Challenge assumptions, question ideas.

- Make decisions by identifying which alternative aligns with your vision.

- Go and get it. Articulate strategy, define tactics, set goals and measure how you are doing.

THREE

BEHIND THE BADA BING: MAKING DECISIONS

Decisiveness

Leaders make hundreds, even thousands, of decisions a day. It is vital that leaders be decisive. They cannot shy away from tough decisions, nor can they go back on a decision once it's been made. Tony sees decisions clearly and makes them quickly. That's why he is able to work so fast, and that's why his company is agile. He is decisive even when he doesn't have as much information as he would like. And he prioritizes. When he's on the phone at the Bada Bing and a call comes through that can't wait, he doesn't hesitate, just moves on to the emergency. And he sticks with his decisions. He gets a lot of flack for making Gigi Cestone a captain instead of Ralph, but he stands by his decision.

Decisiveness combines art and science, information and execution. In order to make good decisions and make them fast, leaders must listen and communicate well. In order to implement decisions well, they must act swiftly and delegate effectively.

Leaders Listen

CEOs spend over half their time listening to others. Sam Walton urges leaders to "Listen to everyone in your company, and figure out ways to get them talking."[1] Just watch Tony. He's always getting reports, chatting, talking on the phone: listening.

Of all the forms of communication, effective listening may be the rarest and most important. Leaders listen well, because they set aside enough time to have conversations, in settings that are conducive to talking and listening. Where is as important as when. For example, if you need to have a long talk with someone, try the coffee shop downstairs rather than the water fountain or an office where there are constant interruptions.

Good leaders understand that there's more to listening than the words that are being spoken. Listen for intonation and nonverbal clues and watch body language for insights into a person's true thoughts and feelings.

Good leaders listen attentively, paying close attention to what is being said, making eye contact, confirming they understand. Leaders know how to listen empathetically, which means they hear the whole message, without judging, and are able to put themselves in the speaker's shoes. Leaders also listen analytically, looking for relevant facts and seeking quantitative information rather than qualitative or emotional measures during a decision.

Good leaders listen inclusively, coaching others, guiding conversations, and putting together different pieces of information from diverse sources.

Of course, Tony is not always the world's greatest listener. Too often he doesn't listen attentively, thinks he knows what people are going to say before they've said it, or doesn't give others time to talk. On a bad day, talking to Tony is like talking to a brick wall. But at his best he is a good listener and enabler of communication, such as when Johnny Sack complains about Ralph, and Tony makes a bid for communication: "At least hear Ralph out."

Perhaps most importantly, effective leaders listen to creativity and innovation. Tony is always on the lookout for the next new idea, and he'll listen to anyone who might have it. IBM CEO Sam Palmisano is known for seeking out innovative ideas from every corner of the company, as well as from consumers. "The technology companies that succeed will be those that have developed skills at listening and a sophisticated understanding of their customers' industries," Palmisano says.[2]

Leaders Communicate Well

"We are learning how to communicate," Tony says. He knows the importance of good communication. Good communication is the lifeblood of any relationship or organization. And communication takes many forms, including writing, speaking and listening.

Part of deciding well is communicating well. And part of good communication is choosing the most effective form, the right medium for the message. If you need to question a decision, or comment on someone's behavior in this morning's meeting, a frank one-on-one chat will probably work best. If you're asking or answering a quick question, use email. Need something more permanent? Try a letter or memo. And remember, communicating faster saves time. If you can condense that email, do so. Find ways to make reports more concise, and you'll save everyone some time.

Good communication means understanding the audience, choosing the right means of communication and simplifying the message. When Tony gives the befuddled Christopher an ultimatum about going to Hollywood, he speaks to him one-on-one and spells it out in no uncertain terms.

Tony is clear about what he wants to say—and why. He always delivers the message succinctly, although most managers find it unnecessary to add the Tony Soprano punctuation at the end of a message—a shove, punch or vise-like grip applied to the testicles. Because they are direct, Tony and his crew usually pose a simple question to ensure that their message has been heard. "Understand me?" Tony asks Big Pussy after a frank chat. "What'd I say?" Christopher asks Jackie Jr. after relaying a decision.

Effective communication is fast, direct, targeted to the right audience and utilizes the appropriate medium, whether the message is good or bad. Don't sugarcoat bad news beyond recognition and don't avoid telling the person who will be hardest hit by bad news. When Gigi is promoted to captain over Ralph, what does Tony do? He tells Ralph.

Effective leadership means leading conversations, getting the right people in the right room and getting them to talk. Leaders not only communicate well, they enable communication. And good communication means making sure your message has been heard and that your organization is communicating effectively internally as well as getting important messages to key external audiences. The larger the audience and the more complex the message, the more difficult those communications become.

Effective leadership also means ensuring the flow of communication, making sure communication goes two ways, top-down and bottom-up.

■ **WORKSHEET** ■
Effective Communication

Do you communicate well? How do you know if you have communicated clearly? Here's the Tony Soprano primer for effective communication.

Know what you want to say. Are you clear about what you want to communicate?

_____

_____

Know your audience. Have you identified the right audience? Do you know your audience's communication needs?

_____

_____

Look and listen. Do you maintain eye contact, listen, take notes, ask questions if something is unclear?

_____

_____

The medium is the message. What is the best way to communicate this particular piece of information—phone call, meeting, email, memo?

_____

_____

Language is the tool of communication. Do you use language that is clear and precise?

_____

_____

Structure your message. Do you organize your thoughts carefully?

_____

_____

Stand up, speak up, shut up. Do you deliver the message clearly and concisely?

_____

_____

Follow through. Do you take steps to ensure that your message has been understood?

_____

_____

Decide Well

Here's Tony on decisiveness: "A wrong decision is better than indecision." And he practices what he preaches. When his uncle's team threatens one of Tony's people, he takes action, sends them a message. Not weeks or days later—hours later. Tony makes tough decisions and makes them fast. And he is willing and able to take responsibility for his decisions.

Although decisions must be made fast and constantly, the right decision has many building blocks, among them the ability to see the future and think strategically, the capacity to listen and communicate effectively, and an aptitude for execution.

It is because Tony has an unfaltering sense of his business and the leadership ability to communicate and get things done that he is able to make decisions fast and ensure that they are executed well. Only rarely, only when a situation is very complicated, do you hear Tony say that he needs to think about something for a while, and even then, he usually has an answer—and a specific action plan—within a day. For example, he weighs the dangers of clipping the boss of a New York crime family and decides against the hit. Sure, Tony sometimes goes back on what he's decided (especially in light of new evidence), and he often analyzes a decision more carefully after the fact to make sure he reached the right decision. Sometimes a leader can go back on a decision; a lot of times he can't. Tony knows that he can't undo making Gigi a captain over Ralph, and Uncle Junior confirms his fear, saying it sends the wrong message: "That you're indecisive and unsure of yourself."

Uncle Junior may know what is and isn't decisive, but he's a theoretician not a practitioner. Junior equivocates. He gives an order, then changes his mind. He cowers in the backseat of his Lincoln Town Car while his soldier caps someone, uncertain if he's made the right decision. Good leaders try to make the right decision most of the time, but they make *a* decision all of the time. They don't hide when they make a difficult decision, and they don't spend their lives looking over their shoulders.

BE DECISIVE

Never postpone vital decisions. Decisiveness is one of the most important qualities of a good leader. A system for action planning helps increase decisiveness and enables proactive solutions:

➤ Set specific goals; ask specific questions.

➤ Gather evidence and information to reach an informed decision.

➤ Speak to experts, interested parties, team members.

➤ Define needs and responsibilities.

➤ Make action plans and timetables.

➤ Forecast outcomes.

➤ Decide.

➤ Implement.

➤ Evaluate.

Warp Speed

The right decision is only valuable if it is made fast and implemented well. According to the Tony Soprano approach, successful implementation is equal parts getting things done well and getting them done fast.

The problem is: we're already working fast. Americans work harder today than in any other period of history. Putting in extra hours is not really an option. We're all strapped for time. Everyone works more; everyone multitasks. Already an estimated twenty-four million Americans work around the clock in the growing "24/7 culture."[3] Take a look at Tony's life. He runs a multimillion-dollar business, yet he finds time to have a mistress, go drinking with the boys, hang out at the Bada Bing or sleep until noon. That's because when he works, he works fast. He reaches decisions fast, delegates quickly, and he rarely has time for a

■ **WORKSHEET** ■
Reach the Right Decision

Leaders make hundreds of decisions every day. Diagnosing problems correctly and reaching the right decision quickly are crucial to any organization. Use this worksheet to make faster, smarter decisions.

Understand the decision. Why does it need to be made? Think about resources, opportunities, timing, negotiations, people.

_____

_____

_____

Identify the problem.

_____

_____

_____

Prepare to decide. Have you looked at all the issues involved? Are you looking at the issues objectively or emotionally? Do you have all the information you need?

_____

_____

_____

Find out where you are. What's been done to date? Where do things stand?

_____

_____

_____

Who is participating in the decision? Should you consult others? Who and why?

_____

_____

_____

Use SWOT analysis (Strengths, Weaknesses, Opportunities, Threats).

_____

_____

_____

What are the effects different decisions may have?

_____

_____

_____

Review forecasts, question assumptions, check models.

_____

_____

_____

Generate ideas, solutions, alternatives, options.

_____

_____

_____

Decide where you want to be.

_____

_____

_____

Have you considered best- and worst-case scenarios?

_____

_____

_____

Select and discard ideas you have considered.

_____

_____

_____

Articulate the risks and trade-offs.

_____

_____

_____

If the solution or decision still passes muster, then implement.

_____

_____

_____

Commit and communicate. Make sure that others share your commitment and have received the right message.

_____

_____

_____

Review the decision, its actions and consequences. Check against forecasts. Was it the right decision? If not, why not?

_____

_____

_____

long meeting. Instead, he chooses a focused sitdown to resolve issues. When he's on a business trip, he works. When he drives in his car, or when Christopher or Furio is driving him to a meeting, he's working. Even when he is at the Bada Bing, he's working—talking on the phone, setting up meetings, negotiating, checking in.

One of the many rewards of Tony's speed and efficiency is that when he is home, he devotes himself to home and family. You never see him lugging a pile of documents home at the end of the day, nor do you see him at the kitchen table with a laptop or spreadsheet. As Tony demonstrates, saving time on one thing allows leaders to use that time elsewhere—and benefits accrue.

They say time is the new money. We want more of it, try to spend it wisely, and work to save it. In order to save time, leaders must decide fast, act fast and learn fast. Leaders are forced to respond to problems, adopt new processes and technologies and manage shifting teams, often across borders or via virtual channels. Tony is able to act quickly in part because he is a keen observer of people and a good anticipator of thoughts, behaviors and outcomes. His ability to intuit the feelings of people around him and anticipate actions makes Tony a more efficient leader.

Good leaders prioritize, effectively moving time from less important to more important tasks. And they become adept at reshuffling priorities. If there's a meeting you don't need to attend, skip it and do something that can't wait. If you're on a plane, get that memo written. The time saved may be used for personal coaching of a new employee or tossing a football with the kids (or playing video games if they're anything like A.J.).

Tony expects others to be fast too. When someone takes too long completing an assignment or arrives late for a meeting, Tony gets annoyed. Sure, he's impatient, but businesses must run on time, and Tony knows that. If Tony had favorite management mantras, one of them would probably be "fast and steady."

Lorenzo Zambrano, CEO of cement giant Cemex, has moved fast to bring technology into the cement business, fold in new ventures, build e-commerce channels, improve inventory systems and increase distribution. At the heart of Zambrano's innovation is the rapid deployment of an IT network that manages every aspect of the company's business, from trucks to tracking. "We're early adopters of leading-edge technology," Zambrano says. And the result? The wired cement giant is a seven billion dollar global giant.[4]

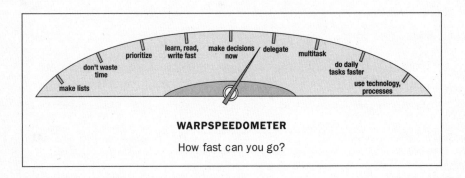

WARPSPEEDOMETER

How fast can you go?

■ WORKSHEET ■
Use Time Wisely

Time is a manager's most valuable resource. Analyzing, understanding and planning your time will make you more efficient. Do you use your time wisely? How many ways do you save time and increase efficiency?

Prioritize tasks. Do you set aside time every day to review and prioritize how you will spend your time?

_____

_____

List. Do you make lists of things you need to do? What are the three most urgent things on tomorrow's list? Have you listed so many things that you can't possibly get them all done? (Not a good idea.)

_____

_____

Balance. Do you divide your day into urgent tasks that must be attended to immediately, daily business items that you will do for most of the day and non-urgent tasks that you can get to when time allows?

_____

_____

The hardest part of any project is starting. When you get a new assignment or project, do you segment tasks, identify the piece that you should begin with and start work on that immediately?

_____

_____

Say no. Do you close the door, take the phone off the hook, keep away from emails for periods of time while you get important things done?

_____

_____

Delegate. Do you delegate or delete tasks in order to save time?

_____

_____

Be more efficient. Are there daily tasks you could accomplish in less time?

_____

_____

Skim, then dig. Do you skim memos and emails initially, then give them a closer read later if necessary?

_____

_____

Plan. Do you plan the day ahead during your commute to work?

_____

_____

Budget your hours. Do you split your working day into thirty- or sixty-minute chunks and keep a log of how you spend your time?

_____

_____

Review. Do you review your time log?

_____

_____

Save time to think. Do you schedule time for strategic thinking?

_____

_____

Estimate. Do you estimate how long a task will take, then check back to find out if your estimate was correct?

_____

_____

On time saves time. Do you get to meetings on time and well prepared and insist that others do the same?

_____

_____

Brevity saves time. Do you limit the duration of phone calls and emails?

_____

_____

Grouping tasks saves time. Do you store emails, then devote a chunk of time to answering them all?

_____

_____

Use technology, processes. What software applications or processes could you use to save time?

_____

_____

Leaders Enable Change

Vision + Decision = Change. Decisions large and small are the catalysts of change. Leaders make decisions in order to navigate companies or teams through transformations. Leaders must plan ahead, combining strategy based on smart vision with the right tactical plan. Effective leadership means that you not only manage change but also encourage others to generate new ideas.

Tony has changed the structure and focus of his company, from a traditional mobster portfolio to a diverse mix of businesses that includes real estate and stock brokerage. He does all of this because it fits his vision of the future, and he manages change by adopting new systems, handing out new responsibilities, forging new alliances, making commitments and restructuring. Under Tony's watchful eye, the business is moving into safer, more profitable ventures and away from some outdated business practices. No doubt about it, the going is tough. That's why he's busy.

THE WRAP-UP

Leadership is all about making smart, fast decisions and then implementing them well.

- Leaders make lots of decisions. Deciding fast and deciding well are vital skills the effective leader must master.

- Don't run away from tough decisions.

- Listen well, enable conversation and communicate well. These skills will help you to learn, decide and execute.

- Act decisively. Most decisions cannot wait because there are a hundred more waiting in the wings.

- Commit and communicate. Make sure others are committed to your ideas and understand your decisions.

- Implement decisions effectively and efficiently. Any decision is only as good as its implementation.

- Stick with your decisions (but be willing to accept a mistake when you make one).

- Transformation comes about as a result of smart vision and coherent decisions.

FOUR

BUSTING BALLS AND BUILDING TEAMS

Your Crew Is Everything

In most organizations, a lot of work gets done by teams or groups. That's because groups pull together individual talents, facilitate communication and enable collaboration. It is the job of the leader to build and organize groups, motivate their members, make sure they have the resources they need, and foster a sense of responsibility and accountability. Of course, every group is made up of individuals, and the leader must balance the needs and motivations of the individual with the goals of the team. If groups do not work harmoniously, their energy turns inward and they erupt in clashes of personalities or ideas, quickly spiraling toward dysfunction and dissolution.

Team Building 101

A successful team begins with a successful leader. Tony has three leadership characteristics that get people on his side and get the results he wants:

- He's *credible:* His successes speak for themselves, his people believe in him. He is trustworthy and smart, and his actions, while sometimes harsh, are rarely capricious or whacko.

- He favors *cooperation not competition:* Tony builds team spirit, fosters togetherness and mutual trust. He knows the competition is ruthless and work can be tough, so he helps his crew to pull together and work as a team, all of which make him a good guy to follow.

- He emphasizes *learning and profit:* Work for Tony and you'll learn about the business, learn what areas are safer than others, how to maximize margins and minimize risk. And you'll make money.

Team builders lead by creating energy, coaching talent, enabling collaboration and motivating people. Good leaders put teams together, solve problems and help groups to collaborate better and work more efficiently. Tony does not lead by micromanaging. He's a captain, not a controller. He delegates fully, knows when and how to step back and makes sure the team operates as a group, not as an extension of its leader. Most of the time Tony sets up a team, then gets out of the way.

A successful team is the sum of its parts: a team is multiple relationships. Tony is good at fostering trust and understanding to ensure that the team coheres and collaborates.

Build the Right Team

Tony's success as a leader can be attributed to the quality of his team—and his ability as a team builder. How do you build the right team and help them to achieve excellence? By having a clear model of what an excellent team looks like.

A good team has:

- A blend of talents and experiences, personalities, work styles, idiosyncrasies, even shortcomings

- A shared mission and sense of purpose

- Good communication

- Honesty, trust and mutual respect and support

- The ability to work together and learn lessons from both success and failure

- The resilience to weather storms

- The ability to evaluate itself and make modifications

Smart leaders steer clear of team building dangers:

- Don't build a team of all the same personalities or talents. Different members must not be clones of the leader (or anyone else), and their contributions and styles must be different from one another.

- Don't build a team of "yes people." While it's reassuring to have people who like your ideas, it probably doesn't help formulate strategy or execute plans.

- Don't try to control every action and decision of the team.

- Don't build teams that are so big that people's skills overlap, or so overstaffed that they feel like committees.

- Don't build teams according to résumés, cliques, friendships or past alliances.

Hire Well

Tony's crew consists of misfits, murderers and sociopaths. But he works hard to build the best possible team, recruit good people and nurture talent.

The first and possibly most important step toward building effective teams is to hire and promote the right people. Just ask Brendan and Jackie Jr. how difficult it is to become a made-man.

We're not really privy to Tony's rationale for hiring and promoting. But we're aware that he puts a lot of thought into it. He watches carefully, thinks about how people act and react, predicts what snares they might encounter. He can see, for example, that Jackie Jr. is a hothead and a liar, even though he's just a kid ripping off concession stands. Similarly, he can see that Brendan is a junkie who lacks brains and discretion. Neither of them gets hired.

Jeffrey Bezos, founder of Amazon.com, is adamant about hiring smart people. He believes that mediocrity multiplies: average employees hire more average employees. So smart managers must look for two traits when hiring, hoping to find people who demonstrate both attributes—intelligence and drive.[1]

Good leaders are always on the lookout for potential employees, for the right addition to their teams, and we do see Tony recruit talent. On a business trip to Italy, he encounters Furio Giunta, a tough, amiable Neopolitan who speaks English and understands power and negotiation. In Furio, Tony sees a well-trained, loyal employee. And he does what it takes to hire the man he wants, namely agreeing to a lower price on stolen cars. Tony knows that long-term talent is worth short-term sacrifice.

Once he's made a hire, the successful team leader concentrates on training and communicating vision. He encourages innovation and success, whether that means revenue generation, fast learning, or strong support for other team members. Leaders help each team member to find what interests her, to do what she does best, to shine. Tony shows Furio the ropes and makes sure Chris is getting the training he needs, and he monitors their progress.

Case Study

Rayeel, the owner of a small consulting firm, complains that he's always competing against bigger, wealthier rivals to hire talented people. Furthermore, he believes the smaller the company the more important recruiting and hiring become. So Rayeel keeps his standards high, commits time and resources and is open to a wider pool of candidates. His company doesn't have a human resources person, let alone department, so it taxes everyone to interview new candidates. And yet they have numerous interviews and a long process before someone gets hired. He tells his team to be patient: they need to find the right person, and that may take a while.

Rayeel begins with a clear needs assessment. Before a job is posted or the first candidate interviewed, his team works out a specific job description.

The entire staff interviews candidates and decides who is the best applicant. Rayeel's interviews are conducted on a hierarchical basis. Junior people screen the first round. To make their lives easier, and to apply some standardization to a highly qualitative process, Rayeel has form questionnaires to help junior associates interview well. These are logic, background and process questions designed to test logical thinking, communication, critical and analytical skills.

When he's interviewing candidates, Rayeel tries to get them to talk about areas in their jobs where they excel, as well as what they feel passionate about. The latter is important, he says, because it's a sure way to get a good sense of the person, see how smart they are and how they organize their thoughts.

At each step, it's not only the candidates' answers that count. Form matters. They must be prepared for interviews. They should write thank-you letters. They must have copies of their résumés, must ask intelligent questions, dress correctly, act correctly, show up on time. Add up all the little things, Rayeel says, and you have a pretty good test of how someone will work out in a client services company.

When someone is hired, Rayeel's company makes a big deal about it. Because it is a big deal. The whole company will have lunch together in the conference room to say welcome, and within a week or so Rayeel and at least one other person will go to lunch or drinks with the new hire to chat about goals and life outside of the office.

Inspire Well

Of course, building teams doesn't end with hiring the right people. After that comes the real work. Tony has high expectations for his team. They must swear an oath and live by it, obey orders, bring in their share of revenues. In return, he must earn their trust, inspire them, nurture and train them. Tony's not a touchy-feely guy, so his lessons are usually brief and to the point. But he does inspire his team, and he does coach the younger guys, like Christopher and Furio, pointing out risky ideas, what is and isn't a federal crime or violation of interstate commerce laws.

A lot of managers think that there's no time to waste teaching nonessential skills, discussing team goals, taking seminars or attending out-of-the-office training sessions. But, as Tony knows, these things make teams more successful and employees happier and more productive.

Next come raises and promotions, not easy matters. Look at Ralphie and Christopher. It's not easy to become a *capo*. And it shouldn't be easy. Hiring and promoting people are among the most important tasks any leader undertakes, and they must be done carefully and well.

Big Cheese and Chief Squeezer

Tony is a loyal friend to team members. He's also a tough boss. He puts the screws to his captains when they don't earn enough. Putting the squeeze on talent, from mail clerk to executive, is part of the Tony Soprano approach. He piles responsibilities on Christopher to help him learn and grow. He's grooming him. Fast. Tony believes it's okay to squeeze to train or inspire better performance.

Proctor & Gamble CEO A. G. Lafley, though milder in manner than

Uncle T, takes the same approach, looking for an executive who has proven himself—and then pushing him to the next level. "We need to get him in a position where we can stretch him," Lafley says.[2]

Hierarchy and Rules

Tony likes hierarchy and ladders, checks and balances. He's not an open office, flattened organization, hive or lab kind of guy. His office may be in a strip club, but the executives have desks (and guess who has the big one in the corner?). He applies rules to teams, delegates according to seniority, accords autonomy and remuneration according to rank. And he's not alone. These days managers are moving back to hierarchy and clearly defined duties after experiments in the eighties and nineties with non-hierarchical offices and management styles that stressed flattened organizational structures, open spaces, vague job descriptions and few rules. Tony insists that everyone climb the ladder from soldier to captain, and the responsibilities and rewards people receive are based on the rank they have attained. And if that ladder disappears? As Tony puts it, "You don't want to create confusion, insubordination."

For Tony, both leading and learning are based on systems and hierarchies. The Tony Soprano approach to team building, then, means putting the right organizational structures in place to enable the growth of individuals and teams.

A Thousand Points of Team Building

Because Tony wants members of his team to grow and learn, and because he is busy (and impatient), he sets up relationships of mentors and monitors. So Paulie, an experienced *capo,* is Christopher's mentor. He is responsible for training his direct report—and making sure he earns, abides by the rules and learns. In turn, Christopher and others are responsible for the actions of wiseguy wanna-bes. And Tony holds mentors accountable. When Christopher confesses to Tony about a botched robbery committed by his mentee, he tries to pass the buck, but Tony doesn't buy it. "Did you offer any guidance?" he asks. "What do we mean when we say leadership?"

One of the many benefits of managerial hierarchies is the ease with which systems of checks and balances can be built, teams can be made and reorganized, and mentoring can be enabled. Most of the time it works. Paulie mentors Christopher, and the kid learns fast. After one slipup, he makes good on being a made-man. Sometimes levels and mentoring serve to highlight lack of aptitude. Tony charges Christopher with looking out for Jackie Jr. And maybe Christopher is not the greatest mentor, or maybe Jackie's stupidity or obstinacy doom him, but he doesn't learn enough to survive.

A second important benefit of clear organizational structure is the manager's ability to change or streamline that structure. Tony manipulates the structure of his organization to make it the most effective architecture for building relationships, ensuring security and increasing productivity. He moves Silvio and Paulie into senior management roles, demotes Big Pussy and creates a more streamlined, vertical organization that both shores up his power and limits his legal exposure. Good managers know how to structure and restructure companies, departments and teams to make them more productive, fun and profitable.

Helmut Werner, former chief executive of Mercedes-Benz, trimmed the layers of management between boardroom and factory floor from six to four, while making plant managers responsible for containing their own costs. He also asked all managers to draft their own letters of resignation. The result: three years later Mercedes launched ground-breaking new models including a four-wheel drive, minivan and the innovative Smart car, and the unit wiped away huge losses, increased productivity and restored profit growth.[3]

Love Is Like Oxygen

Leadership and love? Tony Soprano and love? While these things might sound like they're mutually exclusive, they are not. Love, respect and friendship are the pillars that support strong teams.

Tony shows unwavering love for his children and a great deal of affection for those who work for him. And, like any good leader, he reaches out when he sees that a team member is vulnerable or anxious. When he hears that Big Pussy may be wearing a wire, Tony pays him a visit and reminds him that he has friends and options. Good leaders are tuned in; they are aware of how people are doing. They know when to ask if something is wrong, when to listen, how to lend a helping hand. They also know how to accept involvement or help from others.

The Sopranos also offers the opposite vision, a view of the vicious, unloving manager, personified by Livia Soprano, the spiteful monster of a mother who chose to terrorize rather than love her children, with destructive, lasting consequences.

LOVE YOUR TEAM

We all crave love. We all have our strengths. It is the job of a good leader to find and nurture those strengths and, in so doing, to show love for each and every member of her team. The people you work with are a kind of family:

➤ Make friends of your coworkers.

➤ Let them know that you like them, what you like about them, why you value them.

➤ Do favors, be helpful, like a good neighbor or old pal.

➤ Be there when people need you.

Stand By Your Team

Tony's team is loyal, and they trust him in large part because he's loyal and he trusts them. No one messes with Tony's team, and he makes that known. Here's Tony on Ralph Cifaretto when Johnny Sack wants to clip him: "Fucked-up thing is I don't even like Ralph. If he was drowning, I'd throw him a cinderblock. But not protect one of my own captains?" Good leaders stand by their teams. Even when a team member may be in the wrong, or when they don't like someone, they stand by him anyway.

Effective leaders inspire trust and build loyalty by proving their own integrity and loyalty. They create a climate of trust and empathy and, in so doing, rebuild teams and companies that are more cohesive, flexible and able to change.

SEEK AND DESERVE LOYALTY

There is no substitute for loyalty. No matter how big or small your organization, regardless of your personal style, you gotta earn and keep loyalty:

➤ Be fair, honest, consistent and forthright.

➤ Take charge.

➤ Trust your team.

➤ Reward good work.

➤ Be loyal and reliable.

Tony not only stands by his team—he supports them. He's there to pick them up when they fall. When Christopher ends up in intensive care, Tony is there. He talks to his nephew, tells him everything is going to be okay, and then tracks down and kills the assailant.

If you stand by your team, they will stand by you, just as Tony's crew does when the feds try to pin the murder of Matt Bevilaqua on him. "Just tell me, T," Paulie says, "what do you want me to do?"

Just as good leaders are loyal to team members, good companies are loyal to their customers. Many retailers, including L.L. Bean, Coach and Innovation Luggage, guarantee their products, proving a commitment to quality and dedication to their customer.

Case Study

A vice president of a financial services company fields a phone call from a client who complains about what one of his analysts said in a meeting. The vice president listens, compares notes about the meeting and what was said. Then, he is polite but takes his associate's side, explaining that the client hired the firm to make recommendations and the analyst was simply doing his job and shouldn't be blamed for being the bearer of bad news, or a tough recommendation. The associate happens to be walking by the VP's office during the conversation, and when he figures out that his boss is going to bat for him, it cements his trust, respect and loyalty.

Roll Up Your Sleeves

Leaders, like Tony Soprano, prove their leadership ability in part by proving they are team players. Many leaders agree that one of the most effective elements of team building is the ability to share duties and responsibilities. Advertising mogul David Ogilvy makes the analogy to a master chef who comes down from his office to work in the kitchen. A good manager leads by example—and pitches in. Many young entrepreneurs demonstrate that they are part of the team by sharing in mundane chores, like taking out the trash, answering the phone, setting up phones or assembling office furniture. There's nothing that Tony Soprano won't do. He does the dirty work—from intimidation to murder—and he does some of the boring work—like pouring drinks at the Bada Bing, or visiting wives and widows. If you won't join in and work with your teams, then they're not teams at all but small bureaucracies. And most of us are more likely to buckle down when we see our bosses working hard beside us.

Tell the Truth

If there's one thing that enrages Tony, it's lying. He hates it when A.J. lies to him about why he got in trouble at school or when Christopher fibs about a botched job.

Good leaders agree on the importance of developing a culture of honesty and truthfulness. It creates trust, builds relationships and saves time, all of which are important elements of successful leaders and organizations. A culture of truth depends on not punishing people for telling the truth, especially when they didn't have to do so. And it depends on the leader setting the standard in matters large and small. If you get to work late because you were out the night before and slept in, say that, don't make up some excuse about a meeting or phone call. If profits are down and the board is angry, tell people. Truthfulness holds teams together and allows them to communicate and operate openly.

Different Folks

We've all worked with people we like, people with whom we just get along. That's when we feel like we're speaking the same language, and working with them is easy and fun. And we've all had the experience of working with people with whom we don't get along so well. At these times, we feel like we're talking past each other, and our styles don't complement each other as well. It's easy to work with people we like and whose styles and personalities complement ours. What's not so easy is working with people with different styles and personalities. But Tony does it and makes sure his team does it. Tony works with subordinates, like Ralph, and partners, like the Russian money launderers, who may not be his first choice. But he puts cohesion above division, and he makes those relationships work (at least for a while).

Management coaches often talk about different personalities and how to build teams that benefit from a range of personalities. For example, some people are imaginers while others are implementers. Imaginers think things through. They like to strategize, juggle ideas and discover new and different solutions. Implementers, on the other hand, like to get things done. They thrive on achievement and seek the satisfaction of completing a given task. Both of these personality types can be useful, just as both types have their liabilities. What's important for a leader is to make sure different personalities complement each other. A team will benefit from having one of each, but too many of the same dominant personalities will erode cohesion and hinder progress. It follows that smart team builders and good team players make allowances for different types.

Effective leaders attract and empower competent people and surround themselves with partners and lieutenants whose strengths fill the gaps in their own managerial repertoires. For example, the two partners of a Broadway set design company are as unalike as they could be, but they make a good team. One is a thinker, a strategist, who likes to figure out projects, thinks about the big picture and enjoys meeting with clients. The other is an executor, a collaborator, who takes pleasure in details and is happier dealing with carpenters than clients. Because of the way they work together, the two of them complement each other. But it only works because they are each aware of—and grateful for—the different styles and skills the other one brings to each client engagement, and they are careful not to step on each other's toes. When Tony must make a difficult phone call to tell Ralph and Rosalie that they're no longer invited for Thanksgiving, he turns to the tactful Carmela.

So, there are many types of people, and they must work together and complement each other in order for a team to be effective. A good team is the sum of its parts, and those parts must work together harmoniously. It's no use having a team of strategists or imaginers who sit around and think great thoughts but fail to implement. Similarly, a team made up entirely of people who like details and collaborative work won't succeed without someone to analyze and strategize.

Some management pundits believe every team needs one person from each of four personality quadrants:

- Executor or collaborator

- Strategist or imaginer

- Achiever or implementer

- Analyzer or questioner

Tony may not map out which team member sits in what quadrant, but his teams tend to have the right mix of work personality types. Tony is the strategist. Paulie, Christopher and Sil are collaborators, getting jobs done, moving swiftly from one project to another. Furio and Ralph are implementers, happy to break kneecaps and go home. They're content to leave the strategic thinking to someone else. And a rotating roster fills the analyzer spot, including Chris, Big Pussy, Uncle Junior, Hesh and Tony himself. Depending on the team and project, a different person will measure results and revise tactics accordingly.

strategist/imaginer	achiever/implementer
analyzer/questioner	executor/collaborator

THE FOUR TEAM QUADRANTS

Good teams have one of each personality type and try not to double up.

Tony works to ensure that team members complement and respect each other. And he's not afraid to bust some balls in the name of peace. He tells Paulie to put his grievances aside and work with Christopher. And he makes concessions for Christopher's fiery temper or Carmela's fiscal conservatism.

Different Strokes

Flexibility is the key to the Tony Soprano approach. Managers adapt their styles to each individual and situation. Like Tony, good leaders will make allowances for different personality types, match personalities and jobs and reorganize teams and work groups so that people's different styles become a help not a hindrance. You don't always get to pick every player on a team, so all you can do is rearrange the team structure and adapt your own role to ensure synergy.

Tony adjusts his behavior depending on who he's dealing with. He's not an entirely different person when he's working with Bobby Bacala, a sensitive questioner, than he is when interacting with Mikey P., a numskulled executor. But Tony does modify the way he acts to minimize stress and maximize communication. He's pushy and tough with Mikey, gentler with Bobby.

The Great Mediator

Shortly after Uncle Junior becomes head of the family, everyone from *cugines* to *capos* busts Tony's balls about the new boss. And it's up to Uncle T to make things right, which he pretty much does. Tony is a great mediator and moderator, making Junior feel powerful and proud, and assuring skeptics that their job or business is safe, that it's all under control.

Leaders must organize teams to be effective, help people work better with each other, and rearrange structures and functions in order to maximize harmony and efficiency. They must also spot personality differences and mediate when there's a clash. This doesn't always mean taking action. In the case of everyone railing against his uncle, Tony reminds them that the decision has been made and that they all agreed on the idea of letting him be the figurehead. He reassures them and urges them to have patience.

Personality differences and corporate clashes are going to happen. Good leaders know how to minimize risk and find solutions that maximize harmony and profit. Sometimes, there may be an innovative solution to a conflict of personalities or interests. For example, Apple CEO Steve Jobs watched music companies and technology companies battle over digital music. Tech outfits built illicit file-sharing services while industry giants tried to dominate and litigate. Jobs had a vision of mediating, and so he created iTunes music store, a legal digital music service that promises to change the shape of the music industry—and make Apple a healthy profit. In just three months, the iTunes music store sold 6.5 million tracks.[4]

Get Involved, Stay Involved

Tony doesn't phone it in, doesn't sit on the sidelines. He gets involved. He's a coach, a leader, a team player. So when an area of the business falters, Tony acts. When someone on his team is in trouble, Tony is there.

When Christopher's drug problem causes him to get beaten up and robbed and he hits Adriana, Tony swoops in. He weighs the options and moves toward a solution—an intervention and rehab. Meanwhile, Uncle Junior, a leader with the heart of a hamster, likens Christopher to a dog with rabies and suggests that Tony "put him out of his misery."

Tony knows that people are the most important part of his business. Leaders connect with their people; they stay involved in their lives and make sure they are working toward common goals. Tony invests in people, and when things go wrong, he commits time and other resources to fixing things.

Shit Runs Downhill

You're only as good as your crew, and the only way to achieve that winning strategy is with a winning team. At the same time, "shit runs downhill," as Tony likes to say, and it's wise managerial counsel when it comes to building teams. Because while you may not always lead teams to feats of greatness, you can certainly handicap them through poor judgment and mismanagement.

THE WRAP-UP

Team building, like so many aspects of successful leadership, is about trust, decisiveness and good decision making.

- You're only as good as your crew.

- Hire well.

- Inspire your team to be more creative, efficient and cohesive.

- Build teams and manage people by nurturing, not terrorizing. Don't do what Livia does.

- Love your team. Stand by your team.

- Don't cramp their style. Put the right team together, then get out of their way.

- Roll up your sleeves: Don't think you're exempt from heavy lifting or drudgery. Get involved in day-to-day stuff, even if it's boring.

- Tell the truth and create a climate of truthfulness.

- Build teams that consist of complementary players working together well.

- Figure out personality differences and make allowances for them.

- Be a good friend to your teammates.

FIVE

WHO DOES WHAT: HOW TO DELEGATE

If the Bada Bing Could Talk

Management is all about people. Tony Soprano is a successful manager not because he's a bully but because he develops strong relationships and delegates effectively. The three Rs of the Tony Soprano approach to delegating are:

- *Relationships:* Enable and foster a good interpersonal relationship with each team member.

- *Responsibility:* Take responsibility for functions that should be yours; delineate and delegate the responsibilities of others. Allow people to own projects and give them autonomy and trust.

- *Respect:* Respect the people you work with, and earn their respect. As Tony says, "Those who want respect give respect."

It's the Relationship, Stupid

Tony knows that relationships are the cornerstone of every business. His business is a network of relationships that encompasses family, team, clients, friends, partners, politicians, cops on the take and so on. And it's all intensely personal—a network made of strong, personal relationships.

Many of the people on Tony's team are old friends. But whether team members and partners are old buddies, industry pals or new hires, Tony makes friends, becomes personally involved, knows about their private lives, interests, families. He talks to Christopher about life and love, knows about Paulie's mom and Hesh's hobbies. Tony's employees' needs and goals are as important as any task they are given.

Tony builds his network of relationships by spending time with team members, hanging out at the Bada Bing, going to restaurants, inviting them to his home. And you don't have to go to a strip club. There are many other ways to build strong relationships and foster a personal rapport with key team members and new employees. Many Fortune 500 CEOs have lunch once a month, or once a week, with a cross-section of company employees; others eat in the company cafeteria every day so that they get to know people. During his twelve-year tenure as president of the Coca-Cola Company, Donald Keough ate breakfast in the company cafeteria every day. "It's an informal way to cut through hierarchy," he says. "People always have an interesting response to questions like 'How are things?' or 'What worries you?'"

Studies show that when there is a strong relationship between team members or between manager and worker, people feel involved and perform better. Tony knows that personal relationships provide motivation and cohesion, and he has a strong personal relationship with every member of his team.

.Good leaders don't wait to foster relationships; they don't wait to lead. They get involved in all phases of hiring, promoting and team building. Many take the time to meet with each new employee, or chat with anyone who gets a raise or is relocated from another office. Shortly after Bobby Bacala is promoted to captain, Tony has a meal with him. Similarly, when Chris is released from a detox clinic, Uncle T is there, checking in, seeing if he's okay, finding out which of the twelve steps he's on.

Responsibility

Successful delegating begins with taking responsibility for your own portfolio. Tony is a believer in knowing your duty and accepting responsibility. For example, he personally takes care of a former made-man who flipped, even though Christopher volunteers for the job. Tony has an old score to settle, and it has nothing to do with Christopher. "This is my thing," he tells his nephew.

Responsibility means knowing what you should not do, just as much as knowing what duties are yours. The effective manager knows when she should delegate rather than, say, hire a freelancer. When a company or organization will gain a core competency by delegating—and learning—the effective manager keeps the project in house. In Tony's case, when a situation is personal, like when Silvio and Artie want to bring in professionals to deal with Meadow's soccer coach, Tony rejects the idea of "hired help."

Of course Tony can't—and shouldn't—do everything himself. If he doesn't delegate, he will run out of time, sacrifice vision, diminish morale and generally hamstring his business. He needs to delegate, and he does so well. Each *capo* has a distinct area of operation for which he is responsible. For example, Sil is in charge of the Bada Bing, and Tony doesn't interfere. He helps, discusses the club with Sil, but he doesn't stick his nose in or offer unsolicited advice. With soldiers and *cugines,* Tony delegates on a more modular level, and he allows *capos* to delegate to the more junior men.

And when Tony delegates, he gives full responsibility. When he promotes Gigi to captain instead of Ralph, Tony supports Gigi's decisions, even when he picks the sickly "Old Man" Baccalieri to do a hit. Tony refuses to undermine his new captain's authority by "cutting his balls off." Tony knows that delegation must be decisive and unequivocating. Good leaders don't make decisions with the intention of going back on them, and they don't delegate with the idea that they can rescind assignments.

Respect

Respect is integral to building good relationships and delegating effectively. Tony and his team show respect for each other, their suppliers, partners and clients, competitors, even the cops and feds. It's no coincidence that the mob term for the kind of intimidation they wield is "respect." As in wiseguys shake down corner stores for some "respect." And "paying tribute" means offering a token of respect, usually cash, usually a cut of the deal, usually paid to the boss.

Good leaders give and get respect. They defer to their top team, listen to the guy who was hired yesterday and respect the client's wishes.

Each relationship, team, office floor and organization should be built upon respect and honesty. And when Tony doesn't get the respect he's due? He busts balls. When Christopher questions a decision, Tony snaps: "Where'd you get the balls to question my leadership?" And soon Chris backs down.

Tony, his crew and other mobsters respect each other, and they demand respect. Not surprisingly, lack of respect is often met with violence, like when Christopher shoots a bakery clerk in the foot because he's not sufficiently deferential. For the rest of us, not showing respect, while not fatal, results in not being given respect—and a downward spiral of relationship erosion and diminishing trust.

Prepare to Delegate

Delegation, like combat, is 90 percent preparation. It takes time, honesty and consummate skill. But unlike combat, if you get it right, everyone wins.

Take the Time

You don't see Tony doing many things slowly. He does, however, take the time to delegate effectively. Like other good leaders, when he's at his best Tony doesn't bark orders but takes the time to explain not just how but also why something should be done. So, when he points Christopher in the direction of a crooked cop, Tony takes the time to explain that the cop killed Christopher's dad, and then he provides a name and address. And what happens? Chris takes care of business. Delegating well takes time, but it also saves time.

TAKE TIME TO LEAD

Allow time for vital tasks. Take the time to lead, not just manage and work:

➤ Take time for strategy and vision.

➤ Get away from the office to see the big picture and think big thoughts.

➤ Take time to meet with subordinates, to figure out what they want—their fears, dislikes, goals.

➤ Take time for extracurricular activities, whether that's softball, or drinks on Friday nights, or one-on-one lunches with your team members.

➤ Save office time for people. Catch up on reading, return phone calls and do solo work after office hours or at home.

The Importance of Being Empathetic

Tony is not the world's most empathetic soul. He's not the best listener and lacks the imagination to put himself in someone else's shoes. But he's getting better at it, and it helps him to build relationships—and delegate more effectively.

Empathy means putting yourself in someone else's shoes. It means being a good listener. Empathy will allow you to delegate successfully, pick the right people for the job, have better, deeper relationships—and build stronger teams. When he criticizes Christopher for overtly public cowboy antics that will draw attention to the family just when a grand jury is issuing summonses, Tony tries to empathize. He asks Chris if he's depressed and tries to understand his conflicting need for attention and desire to be a Hollywood screenwriter.

The ability to empathize, coupled with real self-knowledge, provides deep insight into others. If you can figure yourself out—your motivations, fears, dreams, issues—and if you can put yourself in the other guy's shoes, then you will know what works for him and what doesn't.

The Importance of Being Observant

Managers often complain that no one confides in them. It's true that people worry about conversations they have with bosses, concerned that they may say the wrong thing, reveal too much. Even as they try to build personal relationships, their titles, duties and the structures around them keep bosses from being "one of the gang." So the smart manager must be especially observant, must notice changes in behavior patterns, moods, off-the-cuff remarks that may provide real insights. Anything that helps you know your team better helps you lead and delegate better.

That's why Tony's eyes and ears are always open. He doesn't run teams as much as watch them. And he is always on the lookout for signs of danger, anomalies, evidence of wiretaps, or undercover cops. Even when he's having a meal with his old friend Artie Bucco, he asks the waiter to get the license plates of two patrons who look like they might be undercover feds.

Tony keeps his ear to the ground and his eyes open. That's how good leaders learn about their people and organizations—and present problems.

BE OBSERVANT

Managers need insight and knowledge, yet people don't always confide in them. The smart manager must be especially observant, must notice changes in behavior patterns, moods, off-the-cuff remarks that may provide real insights:

➤ Look for signs of conflict, bullying, ostracizing.

➤ Watch for clues, like changes in work performance, tardiness, moodiness.

➤ Notice if someone is unusually quiet, arriving late, leaving early.

➤ If you notice something, talk to the party involved immediately.

The Importance of Being Honest

Tony tells people not to lie. "Don't lie to me," he tells button men and trusted lieutenants alike. He demands truthfulness, and in return, he's honest with his team. Because leaders set the tenor of organizations, honesty and accountability must begin with them.

Successful delegation requires truthfulness and trust. When Christopher hires guys to whack New York family boss Carmine Lupertazzi, Tony has only one question: "Are they trustworthy, these guys?" That's the most important thing Tony needs to know about his people, even freelancers hired to give someone the permanent pink slip. First comes trust and honesty, then comes delegation.

How Tony Delegates

Many managers complain of spending $1,000 to solve a $100 problem. Not Tony. Like other good leaders, Tony takes the time to delegate, gives people responsibility and autonomy and allows delegates to do things their way. Even Uncle Junior, a piss-poor leader, has sagacity on this subject, telling the thickheaded Mikey P., "If I delegate, I delegate."

Management guru Peter Drucker suggests breaking down tasks into three categories to decide what to delegate:

- Tasks that do not need to be done at all

- Tasks that you and you alone need to do

- Tasks that you can and should delegate[1]

There are many important tasks that managers do not need to do themselves. Often, these tasks fit better within the job functions of others, or they will help to train younger team members. After he is released from prison, Richie Aprile hits the old neighborhood like a malevolent hailstorm. Tony must curtail Richie's greed and quash his murderous tendencies. How does he do it? He delegates. He has Paulie and Silvio deal with Richie. And he doesn't micromanage. He lets them take care of their delegated task as they see fit. And, no surprise, they do him proud.

Once you know what you should delegate, move on to who, when and how. Pick the right person for the job, figure out what tasks are most urgent, break the task down into clear components and come up with simple goals to measure success. Tony delegates to Gigi—and makes him a *capo*—because Gigi is levelheaded and has a good relationship with Carmine and the New York family, their partners on the Newark esplanade project. When delegating complex tasks, Tony often assigns two people, but simpler tasks, like breaking kneecaps, can be handled by just one.

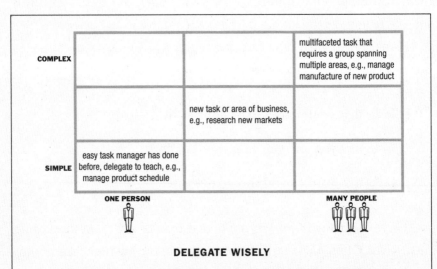

DELEGATE WISELY

Assign easier tasks as tools to coach younger team members, not just to take work off your desk. Group complex tasks and delegate to a cross-functional team.

To delegate effectively, you must keep your eye on the big picture and delegate responsibility, not just parts of a task. You can delegate fast, but take the time to organize and prioritize before delegating, set realistic goals and select the right team or person for the task. When Paulie is in jail, Tony acts fast to delegate responsibility, appointing Christopher as acting lieutenant.

Like most successful managers, Tony understands that in order to delegate effectively he must match functions and experience to the task at hand. Whether the project he's delegating is a major hit or routine reconnaissance, Tony is specific about responsibilities and goals and has a clear dialogue with the delegate about the job. He trusts his own judgment and his team's abilities, and once he has delegated, Tony steps back. He knows that different people have different styles, personalities and ways of getting things done, so he gives delegates room to breathe and succeed.

Trust and delegation are a double helix of good management. Many managers see themselves as coaches, helping to train those to whom they delegate, or a safety net, there for emergencies but hopefully an unnecessary precaution.

DELEGATE WELL

Delegating well is predicated on showing trust and giving up autonomy and control. Delegate tasks that will make a difference, and delegate to a person with the right skills and knowledge:

➤ Delegate tasks both large and small, fun and unpleasant.

➤ Set realistic goals and attainable deadlines.

➤ Draw up a delegation plan.

➤ Provide good training and information when you delegate.

➤ Set goals, reporting mechanisms, milestones for review.

➤ Be available for support, coaching and guidance.

➤ Follow up to monitor progress and problems.

➤ If you delegated poorly, reassess and restructure duties. But reserve judgment until the task has been completed, or until there's a natural stopping point.

➤ Assess the task that was delegated, the delegate's performance and her effectiveness in communicating information and setting goals.

Ownership

We all care more about things we own than other people's things. Good leaders apply this simple rule to managing people. If we feel like we "own" a project, function or client engagement, we think it through more carefully, watch out for changes and details and allow ourselves to be more accountable. And that's what managers want. In return, they must give us some level of autonomy, not micromanage, not dictate the details.

Allowing people to own projects, functions, geographic areas, or responsibilities is, in fact, nothing more than delegating well. Delegating fully means surrendering ownership and not getting in someone else's way, just as you wouldn't want them to get in your way if the tables were turned.

Tony Soprano delegates well, enabling and expecting full ownership. He delegates shylock negotiations to Silvio and assassin hiring to Christopher, and abides by their methods and decisions. Tony considers carefully before delegating, promoting or giving someone ownership over a project. But once he's made his decision, he sticks with it. Just about everyone questions Gigi's decision to have Bobby Bacala Sr. clip Mustang Sally. Not Tony. "Gigi's captain of that crew," he says. "He gave the order. I okayed it. End of fucking story."

Ladders and Lieutenants

Structures are in place for a reason. However flexible an organization's hierarchy, however lopsided the ladder from top to bottom, the ladder must be put and kept in place. As Tony explains: "Chain of command is very important in our thing." And Tony makes sure the chain of command is in place and is respected. Tony runs a hierarchical business. Sil is *consiglieri;* Paulie, Raymond Curto and, later, Gigi and Ralph are captains. Tony relies on his top team and gives them a lot of autonomy and power. As Paulie explains to Christopher, a made-man has only one thing to worry about: his captain. And that captain has only one thing to worry about: Tony.

Many small business owners hinder their own company's growth by not putting a lieutenant in place, someone who has authority over parts of the business. The owners think no one can do it better than they can, and perhaps they're right. Or they reckon if they do it all themselves they will save money, and maybe they will. But businesses need to grow, and if one person has his hand in everything, that growth will slow, and eventually stop. Tony knows that, which is why he has a hierarchy in place, purposely removes himself from various business operations and entrusts big pieces of the business to Sil, Paulie and Christopher, his top lieutenants.

Once lieutenants are in place and ladders erected, it is important that management structures are adhered to. Christopher has this assessment of managerial shortcomings: "Maybe one reason why things are so fucked up in the organization is guys running off, not listening to middle management." Tony knows that when people oppose those structures, go against the ladders or rules of delegation, trouble follows.

Flexibility

Flexible delegation means allowing the players to change while maintaining project unity. In many businesses, this is the norm. For example, at the beginning of an advertising campaign, the account executive will lead the project, but after the launch of the campaign the production manager may take the helm. When Big Pussy drops out of the picture, other made-men are soon put in place to handle his projects.

And flexibility is as important on the organizational level as it is on the individual level. Tony's business changes to meet new market conditions or exploit new opportunities. A tax loophole rewards renovation in downtown Newark: Tony's in real estate. A sporting goods store owes money: he's in retail.

Structure and Standards

Whether you delegate to three or three hundred people, the delegated task must be planned and structured. You should delegate across all people and functions, and those delegated tasks must make sense when put together. The delegates themselves must become a de facto team that can work without you as the fulcrum. The delegated task must be relevant to the person to whom it is delegated, and delegates must be able to work together. If they don't or can't work together, then you're effectively adding a monitoring or communication task for yourself or someone else even as you are delegating to others. It may help to draw up a delegation plan by department or function and look at the modules to make sure it all fits together.

Delegation succeeds when it is monitored and measured. Make sure you check progress to confirm that delegated tasks are getting done and check that there is a system in place for reporting and measuring work. Then, see that there are no gaps, nothing falling between the cracks, and that delegates are learning and communicating correctly.

It's Your Mess, You Clean It Up

When Paulie strangles a Russian associate and stuffs him in the trunk of his car, only to discover that the guy isn't dead and just happens to be a former Russian Green Beret—what does Tony do? He tells Paulie to take care of it. He got himself into a jam; he must get himself out of it.

A trusting working relationship means that you take responsibility for what you do. You earn trust by following through, by making good on tasks and projects you own. You break it, you pay for it. You screw it up, you fix it. And if you're the boss, it's okay to let people know they need to take full responsibility. "You use your own judgment," Tony suggests. "But whatever you decide, you do it way the fuck away from me."

Good managers are decisive, but they also know when to make others decide. Ralph is burdened with deciding what to do about Jackie Jr. after the youth and his gang kill a card dealer and shoot Furio in the leg. Ralph tries to pass the decision back to Tony, but Tony won't have it. It was Ralph's card game, and Ralph is sleeping with Jackie's mother, so it's Ralph's problem. Good leaders delegate fully. When things go well, or when a business unit gets busy, the delegate takes responsibility and should be rewarded. Similarly, when things get sticky, delegates must take responsibility—and make decisions.

Successful delegation means going all the way. You delegate and then step back. If things go wrong, or a delegate does something differently from the way you would do it, you don't jump in and try to fix it. And not every project ends in shining success, not every delegated task is perfectly executed. You learn, you figure out what you did wrong, and you move on. The successful delegator asks herself what she did wrong when a delegate fails to attain specified goals—and assesses her role and effectiveness, whether goals are achieved or not. If there was a failure of communication, or if she delegated a task to the wrong person, or set expectations that were unreasonable, she will learn from the experience and delegate better in the future. As Tony says, after one of A.J.'s school infractions, "You pick up the pieces and you go from there."

It's Okay to Squeeze

When he delegates, Tony has firm expectations and he's not afraid to push until people meet those expectations. Tony squeezes, not for the fun of busting balls (well, most of the time), but in order to achieve goals and make good on his vision—to run a better business, train better executives, maximize profits. He prods the impressionable Christopher, pushes his hot buttons. Tony delegates and squeezes, then delegates larger chunks of responsibility and squeezes harder.

The Power of Persuasion

Good leaders usually describe themselves as coaches not drill sergeants, enablers not dictators. You sometimes see Tony barking orders. For example, when subpoenas are coming down, he whips Christopher into shape, telling him to search for wiretaps. But more often, he persuades rather than orders, inspires rather than commands. Call it the "subtle squeeze." Whether he is trying to get Hesh to reach an accommodation, or coaxing Uncle Junior to go along with a certain course of action, Tony persuades, coaches, suggests. Often he involves others in a decision and discusses options until they agree on a course of action acceptable to both of them. Sure, he sometimes bullies or demands, but he knows that's not the only way to get something done.

Discussing or persuading may take a bit more time than simply issuing an order, but you'll find that people are more willing to go along with your ideas if they feel some shared authorship of those ideas, or if they feel like they had the option of saying no. You can't force people to do things. You can only suggest, and help them to share your vision, goals and plans.

The Power of Manipulation

Management coaches talk about constructive manipulation where bosses influence decisions or behaviors of employees that are in the best interests of the organization. It's a kinder, gentler type of bullying that provides more interaction between leader and employee and works by explanation and persuasion rather than demands and intimidation. When Tony manipulates Chris into killing a crooked cop, all he really does is tell the kid who the cop is, where he lives and what he did— killed Chris's father many years back.

Constructive manipulation, or the "indirect squeeze," should only be applied when the manipulator is keenly aware of the needs of the organization and is steering behavior to accommodate those needs and not personal gain. Tony has a soft spot for Jackie Jr., but when his hapless crew robs a family-controlled card game, kills the dealer and wounds Furio, Tony leans on Ralph to take care of the problem. He doesn't tell Ralph what to do. In fact, he praises the way Ralph has treated Jackie and tells him to go with his instincts. Then he returns the gun that Ralph lent Jackie. After he's sure that Ralph gets the message, Tony moves on to the terms: "More important than the particular decision is that it should happen in a timely fashion." *Arrivederci,* Jackie.

Nip It in the Bud

Speed is of paramount importance to the Tony Soprano leader. And there is no faster way to fix a problem than to stop it from happening. Tony may not know the phrase "constructive manipulation," but he is adept at steering people in the direction he wants them to go, manipulating others toward what he considers positive objectives. When Richie Aprile gets out of jail, Tony tells him to hold off on taxing—or killing—former business associates. "I'm asking you to do me a favor," Tony says. "If you wanna do it, do it. If you don't, go fuck yourself." That's Tony Soprano for a hint.

The Tony Soprano approach stresses prophylactic ball busting. Avoiding a problem, after all, is always preferable to solving one. And that's precisely what Tony is trying to do when he gives Jackie Jr. a lecture when the youth begins dating Meadow.

Expect the Best

Tony builds personal bonds with his top team, nurtures talent, helps to build people's skills and expand managerial portfolios. And he expects the best from his team. After a business celebration in a hotel room, he asks Christopher, "Have a good time tonight? Learn anything?" He has given Christopher responsibility and respect and expects the young captain to make good, to watch and learn and become better at what he does.

Good leaders have high expectations. And most of the time people live up to them. If you work with smart, ambitious people, then you know they are capable of good work, and that's exactly what you should expect from them.

Because Tony has high expectations, he rails against captains who act capriciously or make impulsive, non-strategic business arrangements. Christopher's first real duty as acting *capo* is to manage a profitable construction site. The contract has been negotiated; the job is in the bag. But he screws it up, sacrificing long-term goals for short-term profit. He gets involved in the theft of fiber-optic cable. "Use your head Christopher," Tony admonishes. "Think. The big fucking picture."

Don't Be Afraid to Bust Some Balls

Just because leadership and delegation are predicated on one-on-one relationships doesn't mean Tony has gone soft. Constant meetings to make sure how people are doing, thoughtful gifts and notes, conversations about feelings . . . Hello? Wrong guy. Tony busts balls. He's tough. He, or rather the business, needs to get things done, and it's Tony's job to find the right guy for the job and make sure he does it. Now. And when someone screws up, it's Tony's job to let him know—and fix it.

Too often managers hold off on delivering negative feedback. They wait, or hope the situation will go away, pray that someone else will do the dirty work. But it doesn't work that way. The Tony Soprano approach is not about waiting or shirking responsibility. When someone screws up, Tony gets involved. Fast. So when Christopher shoots the store clerk in the foot and starts digging up dead bodies, Tony has it out with him immediately. The first thing he does is punch the kid. Now, the rest of us might not be able to get away with that, but we should remember that a rebuke must be just that—a rebuke. Don't sugarcoat it beyond recognition. Tell the person, specifically, what he did wrong and why it's a problem. In Christopher's case, he's drawing attention to himself through crazy, public actions, the type of stunts that call attention to Tony and his crew—and end up getting someone arrested. When Christopher tries to interrupt and explain, he gets a curt "Shut up." When he's said his piece, Tony does listen to Christopher. He listens, wonders if the kid is depressed, asks questions about his personal life.

They share a laugh together, and before the discussion is over Tony has made sure that Christopher knows he is important to Tony and the organization.

YOU GOTTA BUST SOME BALLS

The Tony Soprano approach to ball busting is fast and simple:

➤ Don't be afraid to bust balls. If someone screws up, it's a manager's job to get involved, to investigate and, hopefully, fix it.

➤ Investigate root causes. Is there something going on out of the office?

➤ Don't get too personal. Bust balls only when someone screws up. Stick to facts and quantifiable measures.

➤ End with something positive. Tell the person she's important, or talk about an exciting project.

Management for Dimmies

It's easy to manage the best and the brightest. They're ambitious, hard-working, responsible. But how does Tony deal with the dimmer lights on his team? How does he deal with his uncle's crew, or with people hired before his time, or brought into the business because of nepotism? While each situation and each employee is different, the Tony Soprano approach is about finding the right job for the right person. For example, there are big bruisers with small minds whose job is to protect, to bodyguard, to fight, to work at the Bada Bing.

Case Study

Jean, a lawyer in a Fortune 500 company, has responsibility for three associates. Two were there when she joined the company; one she hired. One of the associates who was already there is not as good as the other two. In fact, he's a slow worker and has made errors on major contracts. The problem is, his father is a friend of the CEO. So Jean is stuck with him. After trying to improve the young lawyer's performance through memos, performance review, even third-party intervention, she finally takes the Tony Soprano approach. Jean finds the right job for the young man. The right job is a combination of a slightly smaller workload, somewhat more repetitive tasks and allowing him to focus on certain kinds of contracts with which he is already familiar. It takes some juggling, but it works. Each of the three associates now works to his or her full potential, and Jean has resolved what threatened to become a sticky human resources issue.

The Good Apples

While most managers strive to treat all employees equally, many complain that they end up spending the majority of their time supervising bad apples. Tony focuses on good apples. Sure, he spends a lot of time supervising the troubled guys, like Ralphie and Richie. But he spends more of his time working with his lieutenants, the people he trusts with the future of the business, namely Christopher, Silvio and Paulie. Bad apples break businesses and systems, and Tony knows he must safeguard against that. Good apples, on the other hand, build businesses and make them better. And at the end of the day, that's the path to success.

THE WRAP-UP

In order to manage effectively, you need to know that each team member is unique and you need to delegate according to each person's strengths and goals. Effective leaders take the time and make the effort to lead well, treat others with respect and manage people and teams effectively.

- Take the time to lead, to think about managing and kindle personal relationships.

- Respect your team members and expect high performance.

- Listen and learn. Be empathetic and observant. Look for signs and signals that help you understand people, see danger coming and predict trends.

- Take responsibilities for functions that should be yours alone.

- Seek out people's strengths and qualities and delegate to those strengths.

- Allow people to own projects they are responsible for. Monitor progress and reward them when they meet specified goals.

- It's okay to squeeze, but persuasion and coaching get better results than bullying and issuing orders.

- Give people room to succeed.

- Busting balls is okay. Don't be afraid to rebuke.

- If someone isn't working out, try a different team or a new function.

- Don't forget the good apples; they're the ones who will build the business.

SIX

FUEL YOUR CREW: BUILDING ENERGY AND ENTHUSIASM

Enable Enthusiasm

Tony Soprano is no cheerleader. He grimaces more often than he smiles; he bullies and pulls rank. Yet, he's pretty good at motivating, building energy and enthusiasm and getting things done. Good leaders are good motivators. They are inspiring role models and seem to have an endless fountain of enthusiasm, which they share with others. And enthusiasm, like dissatisfaction, is contagious: it seems to spread around teams. Good leaders are able to build energy through a combination of sharing their own energy, planning well, being thoughtful and bringing out capacities like integrity, respect and constancy.

Go Team

A happy team is an effective team. So how do you achieve team happiness? To begin with, leaders must build and harness energy. They must set an example and energize others, and when their teams start to lag, they must know how to revitalize them. Benjamin Zander, conductor and management guru, believes that a good leader must be a "dispenser of enthusiasm." Tony may be lethargic at times, but he builds energy and gets things done.

Team building requires skill and subtlety. Teams work best when each member feels he has a stake in what he's doing, when each person feels like he has a voice and his opinion counts, when the needs of the group are balanced with the needs of each individual. Teams work best when there's a team spirit, an atmosphere of friendship, respect, support and cooperation. There is nothing more important than feeling that your coworkers respect you and would go to bat for you. That means avoiding situations where team members are in direct competition with each other, and avoiding internal politics. And it means setting an example and fostering an atmosphere of support. After Christopher gets shot, the hospital waiting room is crowded with his coworkers, each one of whom vows to do whatever he can to help Chris, including track down the killer.

Leaders talk about the importance of a shared agenda, of aligning goals and expectations across a team and organization. Tony Soprano works hard to make sure that people agree on what they're doing—and want pretty much the same thing.

Enthusiasm and Integrity

Never mind that Tony sometimes sleeps until noon. When his team gets lackluster, he seems to have a little extra juice, which helps people maintain their motivation and concentration. Good leaders know that enthusiasm is the fuel of enthusiasm. They help their teams stay motivated by keeping them happy. They never seem overwhelmed, never say something can't be done. Even when they have to work through the night, they look like they're having fun, and they do what they can to make sure others have fun and work hard too.

Integrity and constancy are important, because they give people the vital sense that they can trust their leader, and they don't have to spend time worrying about decisions, second-guessing intentions or squabbling about goals. Tony makes sure that his crew and anyone else on his payroll is enthusiastic and shows integrity. And he's not afraid to squeeze to ensure enthusiasm. What happens when Dr. Kennedy, Uncle Junior's oncologist, won't talk to his patient? His golf game is interrupted by Tony and Furio, and he finds himself ankle-deep in a pond holding a brand-new titanium club and promising to do better.

As we've seen, keeping calm and maintaining your sense of humor are also important, because the leader sets the example. When Tony's depressed, the business falters a bit. When he loses it, others do too.

You're Only as Good as Your Project Plan

Tony plans thoroughly. When he begins to concoct a real estate scam in cahoots with a crooked state assemblyman, he goes through various scenarios and plans diligently. When they begin to act, all of the pieces come together, and Tony's team is organized and ready. As he sets up teams and kicks off new projects, Tony organizes and plans. Only then does he move on to carrot dangling, back slapping, drinks after a hard day's work, and the occasional act of intimidation. Tony knows that building enthusiasm around projects can be tough at times. People are overworked, resistant to change. There are a thousand reasons. But building enthusiasm around poorly planned projects, when the boss isn't completely versed in the planning and execution, is next to impossible. Personality and persuasion can only take you so far.

You don't see Tony working with Microsoft Project, noodling over budgets or revising org charts. He seems to do most of the planning in his head. He is different from most managers, who write down their project plans and update them constantly. Whether they plan on paper, use a computer program or do it all in their head, most managers can tell you who is doing what and when it needs to be done. And it's okay if they consult the chart on the back of the door or pull up a document on their laptop.

Many managers build cushions into project plans—to allow for additional cost and timing. You don't have to tell your team when the new product is due at the client, only the date when it needs to be completed. Project managers don't need to know what the budget is, only what their piece of the project costs. If the boss or project manager is able to manage cost and timing schedules—one internal and one for the client—then she'll be able to make sure that costs stay below their ceilings and that deadlines are met. And in most businesses, there's nothing more important than getting the work done on time and on budget.

Avoid Burnout

Tony watches his team carefully. Sure, he's keeping an eye out for possible snitches, but he's also making sure that people don't get burned out.

In today's businesses, people work hard. It's easy to get burned out, and hard to fix it. So prevention beats cure. But preventing burnout isn't always easy, especially since managers are often unable to take people off teams mid-project, or lighten workloads. What managers can do is make sure the working environment is good. A better office kitchen, a stereo system or on-site meditation classes can help to calm nerves and increase job satisfaction. Advertising agency J. Walter Thompson has a "destress room" in many of their offices.

Managers can also make sure that there's more to work than work. Seminars, training or discussion meetings where the focus is on the team members and their skills, not clients or products, are popular ways to keep people focused but break up the workday. A little thoughtfulness or an imaginative reward goes a long way. When Jackie Aprile is in the hospital for radiation treatment, Tony arranges a sponge bath for him—at the hands of a stripper dressed as a nurse.

Many companies find that buying everyone lunch one day a week or getting a masseuse or yoga instructor to come to the office helps to revitalize flagging workers. Birthday parties, company bowling outings, dinners, donuts and croissants appearing in the morning or pizza and beer when people have to work on a weekend—all of these things are easy to do, but the thoughtfulness is appreciated, and they make for happier people and more productive, happy working environments. Architect Zaha Hadid brings a hairstylist into the office or takes her team on a shopping spree to restore energy and build morale.

BE THOUGHTFUL AND GENEROUS

Leaders must make sure everyone knows there is more to work than work. Thoughtfulness and generosity go a long way to revitalizing tired workers. Sociability and levity help people maintain concentration and enthusiasm. Which of these ideas would your team enjoy?

➤ Buy everyone lunch one day.

➤ Buy birthday presents, anniversary gifts for teammates.

➤ Have office birthday and holiday parties.

➤ Go on company bowling outings or lunches or dinners.

➤ Buy donuts and croissants one morning for no good reason.

➤ Order pizza and soft drinks when people have to work on the weekend.

➤ Sponsor a little league team or compete in office sports leagues.

Finally, good leaders think about people's families too. They include spouses and kids when they plan weekend barbecues or office parties. Robert Moses, the legendary city planner credited with building the parks and infrastructure of New York, invited workers' families to picnics and other social events.

Building Enthusiasm Around Unpopular Projects

Tony is good at getting people to do things they don't really want to do: he doesn't give them a choice. He makes it clear that there's an important job that needs to be done for the company and that they need to do it. He doesn't ask or apologize. That's what happens when he decides that Christopher should drive him again. He tells Christopher; he doesn't persuade him, or explain his motivations, which happen to be honorable (he wants some time alone with Christopher to train and mentor him).

Most managers agree that you can't ask people all the time. If something needs to get done, then you're not really asking, are you? And giving the appearance of choice will only get you in trouble when people say no. The best approach, as Tony demonstrates, is to state the needs of the company first, then explain the task. Expect to hear yes, but listen if someone has a valid reason why it's not the right project for her. It's important on unpopular projects that people know they will be rewarded—or at least recognized—for what they do. Finally, if there's no reason for you not to participate, other than the fact that you are the boss, then don't use that as an excuse. Roll up your sleeves and join in.

Motivation

Studies show that money is not the most significant performance motivator. In fact, as employees reach more senior positions, involvement in their team, company or organization becomes a larger factor in their drive to achieve.

Tony Soprano knows fear is a powerful motivator and recognizes the efficacy of a fat envelope as both reward and motivation. Sometimes he bullies or uses anger to get what he wants. But he aspires to a style of leadership where the leader trusts his team, treats them as talented contributors, emphasizes the positive and rewards good performance rather than punishing failure.

USE BRAINS NOT BRAWN

Managers often resort to threats and hostility to get jobs done. While this may work in the short term, participation will win the day in the long term:

➤ Management by fear results in hostility and resentment.

➤ Be sensitive to the needs and goals of your team members.

➤ Encourage participation: allow people to own their jobs and participate in the way the team or organization is run.

Tony uses a wide array of other motivators and incentives. Paulie and Christopher are rewarded with a first-class business trip to Italy. Every captain and soldier gets the occasional share of bounty to distribute to wives and *goomars*—DVD players, designer clothes, shoes, anything that might fall off the back of a truck. Then there is the ladder of promotion and ownership. With success, time and trust, soldiers become made-men, made-men become captains, captains become lieutenants. In the real world, this system can be equated to a combination of promotions, partnership and equity.

There are numerous motivators that drive people to achieve, including:

- Satisfaction: the gratification of getting the job done, meeting goals, exceeding expectations

- Fun: enjoying a task, team, project or client

- Job interest: deriving pleasure from work

- Recognition: being acknowledged by peers and management, winning awards and receiving praise

- Responsibility: exercising authority and taking part in decisions

- Advancement: knowing that promotions and rewards can be achieved, and achieving them

- Ownership: a feeling of owning a stake in the business, team or project

Motivation and the Long Term

Motivation is defined as the will to act. Motivating people is a matter of inspiring them to work (well, more, better, faster, together). The manager must learn how to influence each team member. For her part, the team member must help the manager find the right incentives, the pathways to increased satisfaction. And then, everyone wins. Tony Soprano tends to use money, fear, power and security as the chief motivators. But his team isn't exactly the most diverse group. Most executives find that their team members respond to a broader range of motivations, including financial reward, equity, autonomy, flextime, travel and other perks.

The good news is that most leaders find that when their teams are capable and hardworking, motivation is pretty easy. Most of us know what motivates us, and if a boss is trying to figure it out, the best way is to ask.

In the short term, blanket motivators may work, like promises of reward for anyone who achieves a certain goal. In the long term, however, it is self-motivation that will prevail. Tony promises a piece of the action, travel, celebration parties to achieve short-term motivation. But he also enables self-motivation, persuading his team to figure out what motivates themselves and go for it.

THE WRAP-UP

We all work better when we like what we're doing. We want to be enthusiastic, and leaders must fuel enthusiasm.

- Be enthusiastic and spread enthusiasm.

- Don't be afraid to tell people what to do. Give specific instructions, and make sure goals or milestones are clearly articulated and can be measured.

- Start with a good plan. Think through different outcomes, problems, dates. Then communicate the plan to your team.

- Set a good example. Build energy by being energetic. Show integrity, deserve and maintain trust and constancy.

- Make sure there's more to work than work. Consider workshops, training, team drinks or dinners, bowling, laser tag, sports, birthday cakes, a holiday party or group outing. And don't forget to include families in some office events.

- Be enthusiastic about unpopular projects to set a good example. Make sure people are recognized and compensated for doing stuff they don't really want to do.

- Find the right way to motivate each person. Remember, money and fear are not the only motivators. Self-motivation and participation work better over the long haul.

SEVEN

SITDOWNS, STANDUPS AND OTHER MEETINGS

When, Why and How to Meet

It's pretty much a rule: the higher up the corporate ladder you climb, the more meetings you have. Just about everyone complains they have too many meetings and too little time. But meetings are necessary, so what are you gonna do? Take the Tony Soprano approach to meetings.

First, when a meeting isn't vital, skip it. Tony doesn't even take a phone call unless it's necessary. If you don't have to be in a meeting, or if someone else doesn't have to be there, then limit the roster. If the whole meeting is unnecessary, then don't call it. Similarly, if you can attend for only part of the meeting, then take your leave and get back to your office. And allow others to do the same. If not everyone needs to be there for the entire meeting, then allow people to come and go. Many managers find it useful to have meetings in other people's offices, or conference rooms, so that they don't have to play the host. If they need to leave, or want to get back to work, they can do so, without having to kick everyone out of their office.

Second, make meetings fast, effective and results-oriented. Once Tony sits down, he's looking for facts and results. Prepare well for meetings and stick to the essentials. Invariably, things come up that do not warrant public discussion. It's okay to table—or quash—those items. Do whatever is fastest, easiest and will save the most time. And bear in mind—and make sure that others know—meetings are about listening, not talking. It's important that all participants feel that their voices will be heard, but repeating what others say, thinking aloud or talking just to hear the sound of your own voice is a waste of everyone's time.

Third, make sure that someone is running the meeting. Tony's usually the one in charge, and he gets antsy when no one is running the show, which happens when he goes to his first meeting in Naples. It's okay to delegate the responsibility of running a meeting, just as long as someone is in charge. And it's okay to squeeze. Whether you're running the show or coaching participants, tell them what you expect from them, articulate rules and set goals—and make sure they're achieved.

Finally, format the meeting to fit the occasion. Tony chooses a sitdown to talk numbers with Johnny Sack but calls a formal meeting to address all of his captains. Just a few of you? Try a personal, informal sitdown. Annual presentation to a big client? Make it formal, big and beautiful. Or maybe a standup meeting or a chat is a better, faster solution. There are many meeting formats to choose from.

The Sitdown

The main management tool in evidence on *The Sopranos* is the sitdown, which is an intimate, informal meeting of two or more people. The sitdown often takes place outside the office, say at Satriale's or the Bada Bing. It's the opposite of a weekly meeting with a fixed agenda and a set roster of participants. It's fast, specific and doesn't beat around the bush. It usually deals with only one issue, with the aim of discussing, weighing alternatives and making a decision as quickly as possible.

When Tony deals most successfully with his team, such as when he intercedes to keep Christopher in line or ensure that Paulie doesn't push the rookie too far, he does so one-on-one. In the time it takes to sip an espresso, Tony gives the background of the situation, listens to the circumstances and arrives at a decision or makes clear his agenda. He hears what Paulie has to say about Christopher's successes and failures since becoming a made-man, then tells Paulie to go easy on the kid. While this may seem like a simple, logical approach to the situation, imagine trying to do it within the confines of a weekly meeting.

Sitdowns are ideal for fast resolutions to problems, quick assessments and decisions, previewing meetings, or fast coaching sessions. They work best when there is a limited agenda, when both parties get to the point quickly, listen to each other and agree on a solution, action plan or decision. They can be one-on-one or small group meetings, with internal or external audiences. Tony has a sitdown with Paulie about Christopher. He also has a sitdown with Carmine to negotiate a compromise on the Newark esplanade construction project.

The Standup

Busy executives find the standup meeting an effective way to discuss an issue and arrive at a fast conclusion—without sitting down. Why? Because people are usually more efficient when they're standing up. They get to the point and reach a decision or make a plan with minimal fuss, formality or time.

Standups are ideal for single issues that require communication, adjudication or consensus but can't wait for or don't require the rigors of a scheduled meeting.

Tony's standup meetings can take place in his basement, in a hotel room or on a deserted pier. They can even take place poolside chez Soprano, beers in hand. Sil and Paulie choose a standup meeting to impress upon Richie Aprile the idea that he should be the one to take care of Beansie, the beleaguered pizzeria owner he put in hospital. They're not really there to discuss or debate, so after telling him not to take a hostile attitude with them, they lay it on the line: "Richie, build Beansie the ramp." End of standup meeting.

Case Study

Karen, the president of a restaurant supply company, keeps meticulous project plans with delivery dates, project milestones and scheduled meetings. When large orders are in the works and there is a question as to specifications or materials, she walks the floor and gathers the players she needs to arrive at a fast consensus. The standup meeting takes place in the kitchen or in someone else's office. They talk about one issue only, and when the decision is made the meeting is over. Karen finds that people think and talk faster when they're standing—and she never lets anyone pull up a chair.

The Chat

Just when you thought it was safe to go back to a meeting . . . the Tony Soprano approach includes a form of meeting that is more efficient than even a standup meeting. Say hello to the business chat. If the standup reaches a decision on an issue, then the chat answers a question. A standup often involves several people, and the topic rarely comes as a surprise to any of them. A chat is usually just two people, and the topic is almost always a surprise to one of them. A standup is fast. A chat is faster.

Many managers complain that they spend too much time talking about details and rules—company policy, offices, vacation days, filing cabinets, carpet colors. They get bogged down with simple questions that, for some reason, cannot wait and have to be asked in person. Unleash the chat. When the topic doesn't really warrant a meeting, don't have one.

Christopher Moltisanti, an avid disciple of the Tony Soprano approach, understands how and when to have meetings. So when Jackie Jr. asks him to allow a friend to continue selling drugs in a club that Christopher controls, Moltisanti opts for a chat. "Now's okay for a chat, not a sitdown," Christopher says. The youth states his case, and Christopher says no. Jackie pushes; Christopher explains his decision. But thickheaded Jackie doesn't get it. So Christopher makes him repeat the decision, nods and says, "End of chat."

Faster than a speeding sitdown, the business chat saves time by delivering a rapid response today rather than planning a meeting for tomorrow.

The Meeting Meeting

Sometimes you gotta have a real meeting. A new business pitch or monthly client presentation means that the team assembles, prepares PowerPoint slides or meeting notes, lunch is ordered, hours are gobbled up. There's no avoiding it, and all you can do is make sure that the time is not wasted. You make sure the meeting is efficient and achieves the results it set out to achieve.

Hesh's meeting with gangster rapper Massive Genius is a good example of the meeting meeting. And Tony does what he can to help it run smoothly. He shows public support for Hesh but doesn't interfere with the meeting's purpose or progress. And even when the participants get testy, the meeting stays on track.

The Conference Call Meeting

Conference calls are usually more efficient than conference rooms. They save time and money, because not all the participants have to be in the same place. Even so, effective managers caution against the formless conference call. Although it's over the phone, you still need to prepare and follow an agenda.

The Videoconference Meeting

Okay, Uncle T might not be setting up videoconference equipment anytime soon, but the videoconference is a cool new kind of meeting—and one we'll be seeing more of in the future. A hybrid meeting, it uses digital video and audio technology so that people can hear and see the person on the other end of the phone line. It may not be the same as being in the same room, but it's more personal than a phone call and more cost-effective than flying everyone to one location.

The Webcast Meeting

Like videoconferences, online meetings, Web conferencing and Webcasts provide greater interactivity than phone calls while cutting costs and saving time. Webcasts are ideal when there is a lot of data to present but it's too costly or time-consuming for all the participants to be in the same place. A Web conference can combine video and audio of a speaker with related slides, text, even links to intranets and Web sites. Web conferences allow cost-effective collaboration and speed product development and research. The cost savings may end up being far greater than the price of a few airline tickets and hotel rooms. Better still, in some instances Webcasting and good intranets can make relocation unnecessary.

The When-in-Rome Meeting

During his visit to Naples, high level meetings about the stolen car trade take place in restaurants and private houses, and Tony is, for the most part, polite, even rather formal with his Italian peers. That's because he is sensitive to their way of doing business and adjusts his personal style and meeting manners to conform to the different cultural norms of the old country.

In Europe business is conducted in a more formal manner, and meetings are more polite than they are in the U.S. Subtlety and knowledge of customs is vital to doing business in other countries. Business is global. It is important to be aware of cultural differences, and to know how to modulate your style whether in Rome, Bangkok or elsewhere.

The Not-a-Meeting Meeting

So you complain that there are too many meetings, or that they go on too long. Maybe they're too boring, or perhaps you don't feel like you need to be there. What to do?

First, maybe you don't need to have every meeting. If you're the one calling the meeting, don't be afraid to cancel if it can be handled in a chat or tabled. Perhaps a phone call will suffice.

Second, maybe a meeting isn't the right format. If you're calling a meeting for no real reason other than to get various team members together, then maybe what you need is a lunch or drinks after work. If you're trying to communicate new information, like a new marketing strategy, then think about other ways to share the information. Some managers mock up newspapers and write amusing copy reporting new issues.

Case Study

The marketing manager of a cable network wanted to present ideas on how to drive ratings for their new prime-time lineup. Her group put together a list of strategies and tactics, but they wanted a fun, memorable format to present them to a cross-functional team, including the CEO and the COO of the company. So her group put on a skit, using shows from the new lineup as vehicles to articulate their ideas. They acted out a mock talk show and a fake sitcom; they even took a commercial break. Everyone in the audience laughed—and remembered what they'd heard.

Purpose	Type of Meeting
Coaching sessions	Sitdown
Performance review	Sitdown
Presentation to client or management	Formal meeting
Fast decision on group project component	Standup
Rapid response for permission or decision	Chat
Project status report	Conference call
Multiple city training or sales meeting	Videoconference
Multiple city collaboration or staff meeting	Webconference
Work problems	Out-of-office sitdown
Personal problems	Out-of-office sitdown or suggest a counselor

USE THE RIGHT MEETING

Meetings can be formal or informal, one-on-one discussions or large forums, carefully planned or impromptu sessions. Getting the right results depends a lot on choosing the right meeting format.

Good Meetings

No matter what the format, most good meetings share the same ingredients. It is the meeting leader's job to ensure that participants are prepared, to ensure clear communication, to keep the meeting on track and on time, defuse tensions and maintain focus. Even when Tony is not officially running the show, such as the meeting in Italy about stolen cars, he makes sure the right people are there and keeps the conversation focused. When he steps into a standup between Richie, Sil and Paulie, he notices tempers flaring and immediately has a smile for Richie and tells him to relax, even offers to buy him a cup of coffee. Tony then says, "Sit down," acknowledging that the meeting just got more complicated and perhaps a standup won't do after all. In meetings as everywhere else, the Tony Soprano approach is predicated on flexibility.

Whether leading a meeting or not, whether it's a formal conference or a standup meeting, keep the meeting on track:

- Make sure that the right players are involved. If a client decision is required, make sure the decision maker is present.

- Participants must be clear on why there is a meeting. Memos that specify goals are a good idea.

- Know your audience. Whether you've met them before or not, try to have a sense of their needs, styles and goals.

- Make sure everyone has done their homework. Your team needs to be prepared to present, discuss alternatives, examine scenarios.

- You get to a good meeting the same way you get to Carnegie Hall. Practice.

- Write a list of questions and goals before starting a meeting.

- Circulate agendas and relevant documents at the start of the meeting.

- Know your own capabilities. It's important that the right people present to a client. Pick people who speak well, are passionate about their subject and will hold the interest of everyone in the meeting.

- Speak clearly. Every time a team member speaks, whether it is a formal presentation or not, she should be clear and concise.

- Keep it moving. Meetings can get bogged down by digressions, tabling issues or sending someone out of the conference room to grab a person or document.

- Keep it simple. Don't digress, don't chitchat endlessly. Stay focused on the goals of the meeting.

- Keep it short. Get through the agenda. Use a clock if necessary to keep the meeting on schedule.

- Make sure there is team unanimity. Save arguments, bickering, even in-jokes, for internal meetings. When a client is present, the team must speak with one voice.

- Everyone should get a chance to voice his opinion but don't repeat what others say or digress into idle speculation or gossip.

- Make sure that everyone is understood.

- Follow through and follow up. Finish by making decisions, listing action items, planning.

Case Study

Joanna is an executive at a magazine publishing company. She oversees editorial meetings, participates in meetings with vendors, partners and advertisers, and presents to senior management in monthly meetings.

Joanna knows that meetings are important and time is precious. She tries to prep her team for meetings by asking them to set clear goals and rehearse ahead of time. With new employees, she usually sits in on a dry run prior to the actual meeting, so she can make sure they are fully prepared and iron out any kinks. She runs a good meeting, and when she presents, she is always well prepared.

So it comes as a shock to Joanna that a new employee, Mark, doesn't listen to her counsel. He speaks out of turn in a meeting with senior management. Worse, even though he attended a meeting prep session, he questions a proposal made by Joanna's team, thinks out loud and asks uninformed questions. During a break Joanna suggests that he keep his dilatations short and simple. Mark doesn't really listen to her. He continues to talk through the rest of the meeting, rambling, um-ing and ah-ing his way through unnecessary digressions.

Joanna applies the Tony Soprano rebuke. She lets Mark know that his behavior in the meeting could have been better. She suggests that he follow her format for presenting ideas and, when he does have a comment, that he treat it as if he's writing a short essay: introduce the thought, articulate his idea, then shut up. She finishes the standup with a verbal pat on the back, thanking him for his contributions and assuring him that she is looking forward to discussing some of the issues he raised, one-on-one.

When Mark doesn't heed her advice in a meeting the following week, Joanna gives him a warning: either follow her meeting rules or stop attending meetings. He blathers and wastes time at another meeting with senior management, so Joanna does not invite him to the next one. She does invite him to internal meetings and continues to work with him to discusses his meeting style. When he has demonstrated an ability to speak cogently and share his thoughts only when they're useful, he's invited back into client and management meetings.

THE WRAP-UP

Make the most of meetings. Be fast, efficient and flexible.

- Only meet when a meeting is essential.

- Be prepared for every meeting, and make sure someone is running the show.

- The meeting must be appropriate for the situation. Figure out if a chat, standup meeting, conference call, videoconference or sitdown is the best format.

■ WORKSHEET ■
Keep the Meeting on Track

Meetings are vital. But meetings can be a waste of time. So it's essential to keep them on schedule, keep them focused and limit participation to those who need to attend. Use this worksheet to keep your next meeting on track.

Who needs to be there? Can people attend only the parts of the meeting that concern them?

_____

_____

Is there a detailed agenda? Do all participants receive the agenda before or at the beginning of the meeting? Do you allocate a specified amount of time to each agenda item?

_____

_____

Does the meeting begin with a clear articulation of its background and purpose?

_____

_____

Do you allow different opinions to be expressed? How do you stop the discussions from rambling, going off track or moving into gossip?

_____

_____

Do participants discuss issues, make compromises, reach decisions?

_____

_____

Is there an action plan based on decisions made?

_____

_____

Do you summarize and recap action items and responsibilities before closing the meeting?

_____

_____

Do you follow up with memos and reminders?

_____

_____

- Meeting well is much the same as communicating well, requiring that all participants are clear on the needs of the meeting and their role in it.

- Make sure team members are prepared, speak well and don't waste time. It's okay to use a clock to keep the proceedings moving and ensure that a single issue doesn't eat up too much time.

- Watch what you say in public. Think twice before you voice hesitations or question team ideas or leadership in a public forum.

- Finish meetings by planning next steps, and follow up to make sure appropriate actions are taken.

- Adjust meeting—and management—styles in other countries and cultures.

EIGHT

HEY, BREAK IT UP: RESOLVING CONFLICT

Leadership Is Managing Conflict

Tony Soprano knows that conflict comes with the territory. People's ambitions, personalities and work styles cause them to butt heads. Someone's in a foul mood; someone else is always a pain in the ass. There are all kinds of reasons and all kinds of conflicts. Tony also knows that these conflicts get in the way of a harmonious team and are detrimental to the business. And it's his job to resolve them. Nor can he just fire someone for being a rotten apple. You don't get fired from the family. If you screw up badly enough, you might get a bullet, but that's the exception. Everyone else is there to stay, and they have to get along, at least well enough to work as a team.

Take out the part about whacking the major screwups, and you have every manager's dilemma. There's too much conflict, too little time to handle it, and too few structural modes of resolution.

If you're like Tony, you're going to deal with conflict, not shy away from it. You're going to become adept at recognizing nascent problems between team members, understanding your role in the problem and trying to come up with quick, lasting solutions.

Most management books discuss conflict in terms of behavior patterns, neutral communication, body language that signals hostility, counseling that reduces it, and the right kinds of meetings to talk things over. Tony's approach is different. He tries to recognize conflict sooner and deal with it faster. He's not as interested in communication as he is in harmony. He wants the problem fixed and forgotten. Follow the rules of some management books and you need several meetings and the involvement of numerous coworkers in order to deal with a minor conflict. Many managers complain that neither they nor their team members have the time. Tony's solutions take less time to implement.

Another Day, Another Conflict

If Tony isn't alert to the symptoms of conflict, isn't fast to instigate terms of resolution and vigilant about upholding those terms, the consequences are usually dire. In his world, if you're not observant and if you don't act immediately, someone might die. That is why he is always alert to the potential for a clash and tries to stop things from escalating. He is adept at rearranging teams or whispering in someone's ear to stop conflict before it starts. He stops Paulie and Christopher from duking it out and keeps Ralphie from getting killed by Gigi or Johnny Sack. Tony knows that to deal with conflict successfully you have to be alert to it and nip it in the bud. After all, the only thing better than winning a war is avoiding one.

You Can't Just Whack 'Em

Even Tony Soprano knows he can't just whack every Tom, Dick or Ralphie who pisses him off. So what do you do when you feel like you just can't take it anymore?

You can't fire someone every time there's an office row. Besides, replacing a midlevel manager costs about one year's salary. As a result, leaders must find solutions other than firing or transferring someone. To do so, they must be quick to identify people's problems, whether it's a personality conflict or a case of burnout. They must also get rid of prejudices and opinions that may cloud the matter. Knowing that you're mad at someone is instructive. But that's just the beginning. Knowing why and what to do about it is truly useful.

Break Up a Fight

We may not want to admit it. We like to talk in more banal terms, about different agendas, lack of communication or scope creep. But let's face it, a conflict is a fight. And Tony's approach stems from this simple recognition. Tony's old school. You don't hear him talking about passive aggressive behavior or sublimated anger. To Tony there are only two modes of behavior: business as usual or someone fighting. And if there are people fighting and they work for him, then he stops it.

When breaking up a fight, you have to act decisively and focus on a result—stopping two guys from breaking each other's bones—rather than a method, such as improved communication. And that's just what Tony does: avoid or stop the fight. The good manager knows that acting decisively is as important with resolving conflict as it is with managing a crisis. After a robbery, there's dissention between Paulie and Ralph over who gets what cut of the take. Before things get out of hand, there's a sitdown. Tony listens to both sides, then adjudicates.

Root Causes

"We're trying to get to root causes," Dr. Melfi says of her approach to dealing with Tony's panic attacks. Like the diligent psychiatrist, the insightful manager will look at the causes that lie behind the conflicts. The three major causes of most interoffice conflict are bad communication, broken agreements and unsatisfied expectations. If the boss (or someone else) can figure out and address root causes, then the symptoms—conflicts, fights, misunderstandings, breakdowns—will go away.

The Blame Game

Good leaders don't always look to blame someone else for a conflict or misunderstanding. Much of the time, the problem lies in their own inability to communicate clearly or articulate goals or boundaries. Examine the seeds of conflict. Figure out why it happens and who is truly responsible. You have to delve beneath the surface of the skirmish and consider that you might have something to do with it. More importantly, leaders must have the same goals with conflict as they do with, say, innovation. It doesn't matter much who is responsible; what matters is the effect it has on the organization. It's the innovation that matters, not who gets the credit. It's having a work environment free of conflict that counts, not who did what to whom.

What About Communication?

Communication is important. Tony is often counseling people to talk to each other or, more insightfully, listen to each other. These are preemptive strikes in his war against conflict. He wants people to talk, to understand each other, to play on the same team. When Jackie Jr. is putting his nose where it doesn't belong, Tony tells Christopher to talk to him, to keep him out of the business. Even when combatants want to make war not words, Tony gets them talking. When trouble is brewing between Johnny Sack and Ralphie, Tony urges communication: "He's in Miami," Uncle T tells Johnny. "They've got phones down there, last time I checked."

And it's not only communication but the language that we use that is important in avoiding, or resolving, conflict. From the manager's perspective, the rule of thumb is "communication not accusation." The way we talk about problems, the way we address conflicts, even jokes and body language, must focus on openness and resolution, not blame and anger. Tony often counsels a captain to think, or he says "Okay, tell me what's going on," rather than saying something accusatory or charging forward before he has the facts. These are his ways of staying away from blame and getting the facts about a problem. Solving conflicts is difficult. You need a broad arsenal, with everything from the right language to enable open conversation, to showing fairness and impartiality, to noticing body language. For example, "Tell me how you see the problem" is a better opener than "So you screwed up."

Of course, when tempers flare, even if weapons aren't drawn, Tony's mode changes from enabler of communication to keeper of the peace.

Communication is fine, but it's harmony Tony is after, and he'll use whatever means necessary to achieve it.

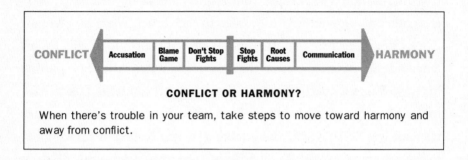

CONFLICT OR HARMONY?

When there's trouble in your team, take steps to move toward harmony and away from conflict.

Yeah, It's Personal

A fight is personal. The combatants are usually pissed off at each other. The manager must acknowledge that things are getting personal and take a direct approach to confronting the problem.

Personal, tough, in your face: that's the Tony Soprano approach to conflict resolution. When a drunk Artie Bucco taunts Christopher, Tony warns him off. Then he tells Chris, "Go wait outside. Now." Tony breaks up the fight before it happens. It doesn't matter that he embarrasses Chris by ordering him out of the restaurant. What matters is that the fight doesn't erupt.

Tony takes a faster path than the one advocated by most conflict mediators. He seeks a swift reconciliation rather than a mutual understanding where both sides take responsibility for what they did wrong and talk about needs and vulnerabilities. Tony wants a workable peace, if not a meeting of the minds. To get there, he doesn't sit on the sidelines. He gets involved early. And he is flexible, modifying his style according to the personalities of the combatants. For example, he's bossy and tough with Chris but an empathetic chum to Artie. And he doesn't take sides. If anything, he makes both parties feel bad. Nor does Tony let the conflict start again. He monitors the peace.

The Group Gripe

Many managers complain that they spend 90 percent of their time dealing with 10 percent of their people. Meet Ralph Cifaretto, a problem child among wiseguys and made-men. Managers try not to take sides against one person in the group, but sometimes there are bad apples, *strunzi* as Christopher would call them (slang for "pieces of shit"). With people like Ralph and Richie, things are different.

When dealing with a bad apple, there isn't always a conflict per se, but rather someone itching for one or making life difficult for others. Ralph is pretty much always itching for a fight, and Tony takes a few steps to deal with him. First, he does not give him the raise he's been seeking. Ralphie is in line for captain and everyone knows it, but Tony makes clear that his fiery temper and abusive behavior are keeping him from achieving that goal. Second, he treats him the way you treat anyone who is always itching for a fight. He keeps him removed from others whenever possible. Third, he does his research. When there's bad blood between Tony and Ralph, Tony asks Gigi how Ralph is behaving, what he's been saying. Finally, he is always on the lookout for a flare-up and is quick to intervene when Ralph screws up, swooping in to separate him from others.

It is relevant that Tony does not rearrange teams around Ralph. This is a tempting solution for managers but is rarely the right thing to do. It is not fair to saddle the most easygoing team member with Mr.

Gripe. Ralph, or any bad apple, should not change the structure of a company simply because he is a massive pain in the ass.

Case Study

Anne runs a software development company. For several months a conflict has been arising between a project manager, Gil, and a software engineer, Nancy. When deadlines are missed, Gil blames Nancy, says that she couldn't get the script written on time, that he pressed her, but Nancy didn't respond to messages and emails. So Anne asks Nancy what's going on. Nancy says that Gil is a muddled manager. Memos and technical specifications are confused and often contain errors, and when he leaves a message or sends an email, the instructions are so vague that it is impossible to figure out what to do.

Time passes. The conflict escalates. Another deadline is missed, and tempers flare. Anne thinks about calling a meeting, getting Gil and Nancy in the room to talk about it, maybe pulling in the office manager or head of sales, someone unaligned and impartial. But the last time she tried that, she couldn't keep the conversation from getting nasty, couldn't stop either side from making slurs and accusations, and there were no positive results.

So she takes the Tony Soprano approach. Instead of putting the two combatants in a room together to talk, she separates them. In private conversations she tells Gil to write specific memos about the project and instructs Nancy to respond to the memos, in writing. Then she gets into each one's head. To Nancy, she says, "I know you're a talented engineer and you've always done good work. But Gil is the project manager.

Gil is this company's link to a very important client. Don't make me choose." Later, when she has a sitdown with Gil, she reminds him what an important client this is. She tells him that everyone else works very well with Nancy, and no one else misses deadlines. "Nancy is very good at what she does," Anne says. "Make it work. There are lots of project managers out there, but not a lot of talented software engineers. Don't make me choose."

She doesn't encourage them to talk. To the contrary, she formalizes their relationship, asking that they write memos to each other until the anger has subsided. She gets personal, even a bit nasty, and she's not afraid to squeeze. She hints at their worst fears: losing a client, losing a job, being replaced or overlooked for a promotion. But she doesn't take sides. And what happens? The project starts to run on time. Deadlines are met, and the client is happy with the deliverables. A few weeks later, she notices that Nancy and Gil are chatting over lunch. She follows up with each of them and they report that their working relationship has improved. She makes a point of inviting them both to drinks at their favorite watering hole after work, and that evening Gil and Nancy talk a bit more. It comes as no surprise that the next project they work on together runs smoothly.

THE WRAP-UP

If Tony were to smoke a cigar with a business leader and discuss how to manage people and resolve conflicts, he'd articulate a few key rules:

- Know that conflict is a part of business and always be on the lookout for signs of trouble.

- Communication and trust are the first lines of defense.

- When there is a conflict, break it up. Stop the fight.

- Separate the combatants, and/or formalize their relationship so they can't keep fighting.

- Try to address causes, not just symptoms, of conflict.

- Be flexible in dealing with each of the players. They have different personalities and will respond to different tactics.

- Don't pamper the bad apple, but keep a watchful eye.

- Get back to communication, trust and a peaceful working environment as quickly as possible.

- Follow through: check in with people, revisit solutions, and make sure everyone feels she's been heard and treated fairly.

■ WORKSHEET ■
BAA (Bad Apple Analysis)

....

Try to analyze bad apples you've worked with and arrive at methods for improving bad apple management.

Describe some of the actions of a "bad apple" you have worked with.

_____

How did you or other group members respond to such actions?

_____

What was behind the actions and behaviors?

_____

Could you have avoided some of the problems that ensued? If so, how?

_____

Without removing that person from the team, how would (or did) you limit the negative influence of his actions?

_____

Were there signs you missed?

_____

Could you have acted sooner? How? When?

_____

NINE

CIGAR TIME: PRAISE AND FEEDBACK

The Good, the Bad and the Ugly

Leadership is about motivation and quality control, praising and reprimanding. Tony is not the world's best boss when it comes to praise and motivation, but he's working on it. He tries to see the best in people and motivates them in a way that speaks to their true goals and ambitions. He also tries to praise people when they do well and let others know it too. He knows that no one is perfect. He understands that people have different styles, different strengths. And he realizes that people screw up from time to time. When they do, he's pretty good at letting them know they've underperformed.

You Done Good

Tony is a miser when it comes to praise. He knows that. He tries to praise people for their accomplishments; he knows he should. Not long after the Triboro Towers hit, Tony remembers to praise young Christopher. "You're doing an excellent job," he says. "Allow yourself to take pleasure in that."

When praise or acknowledgment is slow in coming—or doesn't come at all—people feel unappreciated. The result is they act differently. They may slack off or do things simply to get attention, as Christopher does when he believes he doesn't get the credit he deserves.

Of course, Tony knows that businesses are measured by results, not media attention or a boss's praise. As Harry S Truman was often heard to say, "You can accomplish anything in life, provided that you do not mind who gets the credit." Tony would agree. That's why he reprimands Christopher for his wild antics that seem designed purely to get attention. "Why don't you just leave a fucking urine sample next time?" Tony asks.

One thing Tony probably doesn't need to work on is criticism. He's pretty good at telling people when they screw up or do something wrong.

Speed and trust are essential to the Tony Soprano approach. Whether or not he praises often, he definitely praises and reprimands fast. And he is honest and fair when doling out criticism or commendation. Good leaders keep track of everything that is going on, measure results and provide timely, unbiased feedback.

Getting personal is another cornerstone of the Tony Soprano approach, and he embraces any sort of performance evaluation that allows him to know his team better, to get more personal.

Rapid Response

You can't wait a year to fix a problem or praise a solution. So if someone does something particularly good or bad, react fast. The day after Joe closes a big deal, tell the team. The day he arrives for a meeting unprepared, tell Joe.

Tony Soprano is fast to praise and reprimand. And he knows that no one likes to be reprimanded in public. For example, the day that Christopher Moltisanti becomes a made-man, Tony praises him for his dedication to the family and the contributions he's made.

PRAISE IN PUBLIC; SQUEEZE IN PRIVATE

No one likes hearing that they screwed up, especially not in front of their peers. Every Japanese manager is taught to "save face" in public and save criticism or exhortation for private discussions:

➤ Act like the town crier when it comes to doling out praise. Make it loud; make it public.

➤ Act like a Japanese manager when it comes to reprimands. Make it gentle; make it private.

Praise Where Praise Is Due

Tony Soprano knows the importance of focusing on the positive. Praise is easy to say, and even easier to hear. We all listen to praise, value positive reinforcement, and we're open to any lessons that come from positive rather than negative feedback. Praise is easier to dish out than criticism, is heard better and has longer lasting effects. So go ahead and praise. Do it fast, do it often. Gigi is an anxious boss but tries hard to manage well, and Tony is quick to give him a pat on the back: "Hey, hang in there," he says. "You're doing a good job."

And Tony knows that, unlike reprimands, praise doesn't need a specific time or reason. When he finds himself alone with Bobby Bacala, Tony uses the opportunity to thank him for taking care of Uncle Junior.

Most of us are open to praise, and most of us have done something deserving of praise. That's why performance reviews—and other analyses of people's behavior or results—that focus mainly on weaknesses and shortcomings are less effective than those that focus on strengths as well. Some managers make the distinction between "cop" and "coach," where the cop tells you what you're doing wrong, while the coach tells you what you're doing right. It's fine to work to improve weaknesses, but it's more important to focus on and build strengths. Letting individuals know when their performance has been good and "advertising" successes throughout the group or organization is a vital part of managing people. Managers call this "talking up the team" and stress the importance of crediting staff in front of both internal and external audiences.

One young division president of a large company is known to start every meeting with a "praise where praise is due" segment. There is, he explains, always someone who has done something well, and recognizing that person's achievement is a good way to begin any meeting. Another leader keeps a victory log, a record of personal and professional victories that have earned her praise and recognition. When she's feeling low, or when a big meeting is making her team nervous, she takes a look at all the things she's done right or reminds her team of the things they've done well.

DO UNTO OTHERS . . .

Do unto others as you would have them do unto you. It sounds simple enough, but it's harder in practice than theory:

➤ Don't blame someone just because you can get away with doing so, or because you're pissed off.

➤ Praise people when they do well.

➤ Help people set and achieve their own goals.

How Am I Doing?

Tony Soprano doesn't exactly ask for feedback. But when problems are reported, when Silvio complains that he feels "marginalized" or Carmela reveals that she feels hurt and ignored, he listens. Getting outside views, whether by internal questionnaires, focus groups, client opinion or one-on-one chats is a good way to identify flaws and grow as a leader.

It's important to remember not to kill the messenger. It takes guts and honesty for a subordinate to tell his boss he's dissatisfied with something. The good manager will thank someone for taking the time to provide feedback and encourage her to do it again, rather than defending himself on the spot or lashing out, as is too often the case.

It's also important to remember that if you are getting only positive feedback, you may not be getting the whole truth. No one likes to be the one bringing bad news to the attention of the boss. It's up to the boss to make sure that he's not only getting good news but that criticisms and concerns are also being voiced. As headhunter James Citrin puts it: "The best leaders find a way to get unvarnished feedback and assimilate that in a way that is constructive for the organization."[1]

Annual Performance Evaluations: What Are They Good For?

The word on the street is annual performance evaluations don't work as well as they should. They're too formal and too infrequent, their goals too strict and rubrics too confining to be of any real value. Most managers agree that while the venerable institution has its place and offers some value, it's not enough. In fact, a lot of managers use performance evaluations because their human resources departments say they must. Tony would probably say it's like the traditions of becoming a made-man, or hotel suite parties, or even watching *The Godfather* movies with his top team: don't scrap it, just because it's not the greatest management tool around.

Don't Throw Out the Baby with the Bathwater

So the Tony Soprano approach favors consistent and constant "real time" feedback, and he may not have heard of annual reviews. But he'd probably be in favor of them. Tony and likeminded leaders strive to prioritize personal relationships, and performance evaluations are useful tools to enable, extend and review those relationships.

The performance appraisal is a useful tool to review structure and organization, provide feedback and enable coaching. It works best when everyone knows what the goals are before embarking on a performance review. The annual review should be used for big picture issues. It should assess structural elements like where and how an employee is working, which team he should be part of, when he was last promoted, his salary level. It should allow both sides (employee and employer) to articulate feedback, to evaluate the job. Finally, and most importantly, a review should enable coaching and development, allowing both sides to set goals and targets, establish milestones and identify areas of professional growth that could benefit from further attention.

There are ways that successful managers are changing the annual review process to make it more effective. For example, some leaders who are reengineering the performance appraisal are pushing for 360-degree appraisals that allow review of both boss and subordinate in a consistent, open circle of review and feedback.

There is, of course, no leadership panacea. Although they have their strengths, annual performance reviews cannot be the only tool for managerial communication. Don't try to remedy specific problems in a once-per-year or a once-per-quarter forum. If someone is screwing up, tell her today or tomorrow, not at the end of the year.

If It Ain't Great, Fix It

So performance reviews aren't all they're cracked up to be. What are you gonna do? What do you think Tony would do? Fix them.

First, make them more frequent. Once a year is just too seldom for an annual review to be a useful tool. So do some kind of review more often. It can be informal, but make sure that there are frequent performance reviews, at least every quarter.

Second, don't try to get milk from a stone. Annual reviews are not well suited for providing feedback about specific actions, or inaction, screwups or successes, so don't try to use them for timely feedback. When something happens that requires fast feedback, get on it tomorrow, not the next time a review comes around.

Third, make sure the big annual review contains no surprises. Since management reviews are often used as the basis for distributing annual raises, they are important grades. If you have quarterly reviews and provide immediate feedback when called for, the annual review will only serve to confirm what has already been explicitly stated about a person's performance.

Finally, if the form provided by your human resources department seems antiquated or otherwise lacking—or if there isn't one—make a new one. Get feedback from employees and colleagues, ask friends at other companies about their annual reviews, examine what works and what doesn't. Then think about goals the reviews should address, feedback they should seek, and make your own review. It's okay to add your own assessment questionnaire to the company-wide annual review form. Hey, that way if it doesn't work, you'll have no one to blame but yourself.

■ **WORSHEET** ■
Evaluate This

Whether formally or informally, help yourself and others to focus on positive elements when reviewing performance and redesigning job functions.

How would you redefine your job to focus on strengths and interests?

_____

_____

_____

What task or function would you like to do more?

_____

_____

_____

What motivators work for you?

_____

_____

_____

Do you praise well? How?

_____

_____

_____

Think of the last time you received negative feedback. How did you listen? What did you learn?

_____

_____

_____

Complete this sentence: I am more effective when I use these attributes . . .

_____

_____

_____

What areas overlap between your current functions and your ideal job?

_____

_____

_____

Do people like working with you? Why?

_____

_____

_____

Who do you want to work with more? Why?

_____

_____

_____

What can you change so that you are more effective? So that people want to work with you more?

_____

_____

_____

How can you change your job to make it come closer to your ideal job?

_____

_____

_____

What are your goals? How can you measure them?

_____

_____

_____

What's wrong with your annual review process? How can you fix it?

_____

_____

_____

THE WRAP-UP

Reviewing performance is not easy, but it's vital.

- Focus on praise. Build strengths; don't punish weaknesses.

- When there are specific issues or problems, address them as soon as possible.

- Praise in public. Reprimand in private.

- Review performance constantly and consistently.

- Get internal feedback and outside views on how you are doing, and listen to what people are saying.

- Use performance evaluations to get to know people, discuss ideas and identify career goals.

- Do it often. Make sure performance is reviewed frequently, even if it's an informal process some of the time. Try to do a more formal review each quarter.

- Avoid whammies. Annual reviews should contain no surprises.

- Make it better. If you don't have an annual review in place, design your own. If you have one and it doesn't work, come up with a better solution.

TEN

WE SUCK: DEALING WITH POOR PERFORMANCE

Human, All Too Human

Okay, not everyone performs well all of the time. There are times when people underperform or screw up. Praise is easy. It's criticism that managers find difficult—and they should. It's all too easy for a reprimand to turn into a verbal thrashing. Alternately, it's tempting to go the passive aggressive route, or hand off a problem rather than confront someone directly. Poor performance tests a manager's mettle. Good leaders examine why and not just who and what. They try to determine why good people produce bad results. After examining the causes, the Tony Soprano approach is direct, fast and honest. Sure, you get in someone's face, but you reprimand quickly, with the right kind of response or reprimand.

Mistakes Are Okay

We all make mistakes. What's important is that we admit them rather than cover them up, and learn from them. As entrepreneur and business writer Harvey Mackay puts it: "You can't solve a problem unless you first admit you have one."[1] Good leaders must have a positive attitude toward mistakes, encouraging people to admit them, discuss them and share the lessons they learned. Making a mistake is not failure; not learning from a mistake is.

Root Causes

If capable people are underperforming, there's probably a reason. Maybe they're burned out or have family problems. Maybe they are doing a job that is wrong for them or have been given too much responsibility too fast. It's the job of the manager to determine why things are not going well and try to address the causes, not the symptoms.

So when Tony takes Paulie and Christopher to Italy, and Paulie acts like a teenager on a world tour, Tony tells him to stop and asks why he's acting the way he is. It turns out that being in the "old country" is both meaningful and confusing for Paulie, and Tony arrives at a fast solution, which is to let Paulie be more of a tourist and less of a business associate for the remainder of the trip.

You Gotta Bust Some Balls

Sometimes you gotta bust balls. But it's not easy to reprimand well. Invariably, a reprimand is not something anyone wants or likes to hear.

The Tony Soprano approach is all about timing, tone, having something nice or positive to say along with the bitter pill, and reprimanding behaviors, not people. Some managers talk about "the shit sandwich," where the criticism is sandwiched between more palatable conversational bread. Others try to use a "velvet hammer," which strikes hard and gets the job done, but wraps bad news in a softer package. Whatever you call it, timing and tone matter.

Here's the Tony Soprano reprimand:

- *Act fast.* Don't wait around to find the right moment to tell someone his results were disappointing or he handled something badly. Find a place where you can talk in private, and have a frank, short chat.

- *Choose the right time and place.* The end of a long, stressful day may not by the best time. Try 10 A.M. the following morning. If it's a quickie, an office will do. If you need to have a longer chat and don't want to be interrupted, get out of the office. Go to a coffee shop, or take the guy to lunch. Remember, praise in public, squeeze in private.

- *Don't start with a harangue.* Don't obfuscate, but don't walk in shooting either.

- *Be specific.* Don't bring other things into the reprimand. Just talk about the one issue. Have specific examples of what was done wrong and suggest specific remedies.

- *End on a positive note.* Don't end by saying to a trusted team member that she is terrible and you're severely disappointed. End by saying what she has done well or reminding her how much the client values her, how much you trust her, even how she can benefit from your suggestions. People usually look for what's in it for them, so focus on benefits.

Watch Tony chew out Christopher for allowing Jackie Jr. to get involved in the business. Tony brings Chris down to his basement, where he reprimands him quickly and clearly and ends by giving Christopher a hug and a kiss and telling him, "I love you." For the rest of us, we may not need to resort to basement meetings and hugs and kisses, but the idea is right: be fast and specific when you criticize, and end with something positive.

How Not to Reprimand

Unfortunately, it is easy to reprimand badly. Remember basic rules and avoid easy pitfalls when criticizing, and you'll reprimand more effectively.

- *Don't be the boss who cried wolf.* Don't reprimand all the time. If you are criticizing things of no consequence, it's time to recalibrate your blunder meter.

- *Don't shoot the messenger.* Don't launch into a reprimand just because you've heard some bad news, and don't reprimand the first warm body you encounter after hearing bad news.

- *Try not to reprimand when you're angry.* When you're in a foul mood, you'll only yell or say things you'll regret later.

- *Don't rush in.* If possible, wait awhile before reprimanding. Many managers find it useful to write down their criticism, then put it in a drawer until the following day.

- *Don't be vague.* Be clear about what the problem is, what the negative consequences are.

- *Don't drag up extraneous stuff.* When admonishing, don't take the opportunity to remind the person of what she did wrong last week, what you didn't like last month, how much you hate her new haircut.

- *Don't go too deep or too long.* Don't tell the person what he always does or make pronouncements on his faults as a human being. Stop yourself from saying things like "you always . . ." or "you tend to . . ." A reprimand should last no longer than five minutes.

- *Don't get too personal.* Try to keep criticism focused and objective. Stick to facts, not qualitative or personal judgments.

- *Don't be a broken record.* Don't nag repeatedly when you're making a criticism, and don't say the same thing several times.

Uncle T gets it wrong sometimes. After Ralph brutally kills a woman, Tony shoves and punches, then attacks Ralph's character and repeats his complaints. His reprimand is too angry, broad and repetitive. Even though it may be justified, the poor reprimand fails to achieve the desired results. Of course, you get the feeling if Ralph, say, bungled a sales pitch, Tony's rebuke would have been better.

Guilt Is More Powerful than Fear

The Tony Soprano approach to managing people is predicated on building relationships, on trust and the alignment of needs and goals. It follows that yelling, browbeating and mock executions are not the methods of choice when it comes to dealing with poor performance. Rather, letting people know that they have fallen short of expectations or let you down is a better way to get employees back on track than verbal ass-kickings.

When Christopher's thugs put a stockbroker in the emergency room and cause two other brokers to quit, Tony calls a meeting. Tony explains that the brokerage problem "attracts negative attention" and tells Christopher to "exercise impulse control." The discussion makes Chris feel guilty, not scared. And it works.

Apologies, Apologies

In a particularly harsh tirade, Tony humiliates A.J. and suggests he is not a worthy heir. Afterward, Tony apologizes. "I was wrong and I hope you know I didn't mean it," he says. Good leaders apologize when they screw up. And they do it quickly and clearly.

APOLOGIZE WHEN YOU SCREW UP

Everyone screws up, even bosses. That's okay. What's not okay is to pretend it didn't happen, to ignore it or make excuses. Apolo-

gizing is not the easiest thing to do. Apologize the way you praise or reprimand:

➤ Do it soon. There's no time like the present for doing something you don't want to do.

➤ Be specific. Just saying I'm sorry isn't enough.

➤ Be clear and direct. A p.s. at the end of an email won't suffice.

➤ Make sure you're understood. Don't hint; say it.

Case Study

Jared is head of marketing for a large pharmaceutical company. When there are new product launches, his team works to coordinate package design and advertising campaigns. An important milestone in the process is the presentation to brand managers and senior management. So Jared is shocked when two of his designers and a copywriter miss a meeting with a brand manager because they went out to lunch, had a few drinks and lost track of the time.

When they knock on the door of the conference room, late and smelling of beer, Jared smiles, tells them thanks for stopping by but "we've got it under control" and sends them on their way. The team he's assembled makes the presentation to the brand manager, and the meeting is, if not a major success, then at least salvaged.

About an hour later, Jared calls in each person for a one-on-one. In each meeting, he doesn't yell. Rather he listens to their explanation of what happened, questions them quietly about what they did, then expresses his profound disappointment. He reminds them of the opportunities he's given them, the trust they have betrayed. He's treated them as partners, he says, expected the best, depended on them, and they've let him down. He shakes his head and ushers them out of his office.

Sure enough, it works. Each one feels he has disappointed Jared and let the team down. They change their ways, come to work early, take lunch at their desks, and when the time comes to present the next campaign to senior management, the three are on time for the meeting, having prepared well and rehearsed their presentations.

We Suck

"I wanna know why there's zero gross in this family's receipts," Tony harangues his captains. He's pissed off. It seems that nothing is going well.

Sometimes, the machine falters. And it is worse than an individual performing badly, worse than losing a big client, worse than several people getting drunk or failing to deliver a product on time.

It shouldn't happen at all. In fact, it cannot happen more than once in a very long time. But occasionally, the entire organizational apparatus needs to be shaken up. Egos will be dented, processes will be investigated, numbers crunched, changes made. It's called the "we suck" meeting, and it's designed to fix a systemic problem.

Tony summons his team together to tell them revenues are down: "You're supposed to be earners, that's why you've got the top positions." There are problems throughout the organization, and the implications are serious. He doesn't go into great detail, but he does identify areas of the business that have underperformed, alliances that are languishing. He doesn't listen to excuses, just presents the facts, exposes the problem areas and challenges his team to perform better. "Now that's it. That's all I gotta say," he concludes. "Frankly I'm depressed and ashamed."

The "we suck" meeting is a last resort. It is a group forum for shared blame to refocus energies, reinvigorate teams, reexamine processes, redesign products or services. And you've got to know from the outset that it's going to make pretty much everyone unhappy. There's no face-saving, because it is a public meeting and people will be exposed and shamed in front of their friends and peers. There are no heroes, because the point is: things are bad all over. Sure, it can end on a positive note. You can tell the team, "Hey, we've done it before, now let's pull together and get in shape." But it's not a happy meeting.

The "we suck" meeting doesn't aim to renew energy and enthusiasm—that's better done via a more positive, encouraging approach. Nor does it aim to reprimand one person or process. It's broad in its censure and should be used to shake things up, with wholesale changes in mind, like new processes, increased productivity, better quality control or higher profit margins. And it should be used rarely, if at all. Know that feelings will be hurt and that team leaders will have to work to rebuild energy and enthusiasm while focusing on implementing the new system or procedure. So it's no surprise that Tony resorts to this type of meeting only once in four years. It is a last-ditch effort, a one-time-only meeting.

■ WORKSHEET ■
Reprimand Checklist

Don't shy away from poor performance. Address it fast and well.

What have people done when reprimanding you that is unnecessary? Do you ever do those things?

_____

_____

Who do you know who reprimands effectively and well? Why?

_____

_____

Describe a team you were on where someone you worked with screwed up. What were the root causes? Did the manager handle it well? Why?

_____

_____

What was your most recent reprimand? What did you do right? What did you do wrong?

_____

_____

How long did your last reprimand take? How long should it have taken?

_____

_____

Do you make notes before calling someone into your office? Do you wait and clarify your thoughts?

_____

_____

Case Study

Ellen runs a software company. When the firm doesn't meet projections, she works with key managers to address the problems. When profit margins continue to slip, productivity declines and big client pitches fail to materialize, she takes action.

Ellen calls a company-wide meeting. Only Ellen and two lieutenants are involved in planning the meeting, getting the figures and preparing the presentation. The small team and short preparation time are part of the meeting approach.

The presentation details findings, reports results and itemizes deficits and shortcomings. The next slides are devoted to identifying points of pain—the real problem areas. There are no names, nothing that smacks of accusation, just facts and numbers. Then it's on to solutions, new tactics and next steps for different parts of the organization. There is a lengthy, somewhat chilly discussion, then the team works together on an action plan document, with specific deadlines, phases and milestones.

In the days that follow, departments are reorganized, teams rebuilt. Outsourcing is investigated; functions that used to fly under the radar are subjected to scrutiny and measurement. Some of the executives complain to Ellen. Why didn't she let them in on it? Why pull a surprise meeting? Why air the marketing department's dirty laundry in front of the head of research? Ellen is polite but unapologetic, stressing that the meeting was about the whole company, not individuals, to point out problems and goals common to all divisions.

And it works. The company gets more efficient, time to market on the next product is shorter, and some new deals are closed. The one-time meeting has had the desired permanent results.

Fire Well

No one likes to talk about firing people. Certainly, no good manager likes to do it. Firing someone, laying someone off, even requesting a department transfer is serious business. You need good reasons, and when you do, you should act decisively.

John Paul Getty, the oil tycoon, once explained that over the years he tried to become better at hiring people, at figuring out the qualities that make certain candidates work out while others fail to perform. But he never figured it out. He did, however, improve at recognizing when he'd made a mistake—and acting on it.

Tony Soprano would agree. He tries to hire well. The bar is high, and it's not easy to become a made-man and pretty tough to be promoted to *capo* in his organization. Even so, not everyone works out. Big Pussy and Ralphie are made-men who fail to perform, betray trust, lie. And reluctantly, or not so reluctantly, Tony fires them. With extreme prejudice.

But you don't fire—or clip—someone without good reason, careful analysis and a clear course of action. Some things cannot be undone, as Tony knows when he agonizes over whether to have Big Pussy whacked. Okay, so you're not going to clip someone who doesn't work out, but you may want to think about firing her or, more likely, moving her to a different division, or into a different function. Hey, look on the bright side. Unlike Tony, if you make a mistake, you can reverse a decision.

Even better, you can fire someone without facing a possible murder charge.

THE WRAP-UP

Know that people can and will underperform. Don't expect poor performance, but allow for the possibility, and then act to undo it.

- Don't expect people to shine all the time. We all have our bad days.

- Examine and address the cause, not the symptom, of poor performance.

- Be prompt to reprimand, and when you do so, be fast, be specific and end with something positive or encouraging.

- Reprimand behaviors, not people.

- Don't just yell. Simply getting angry doesn't fix problems. Figure out what's wrong and try to fix it.

- It's okay to squeeze: lay a guilt trip on someone if you need to.

- Apologize when you screw up.

- Firing someone or holding a "we suck" meeting is a last-resort action. Do these rarely, carefully and expeditiously.

ELEVEN

DEAL TIME: EFFECTIVE NEGOTIATION

How to Negotiate with Assassins

Tony Soprano sits down with politicians, hitmen and thugs and usually gets what he wants. Sure, he intimidates. How does he do it? The Tony Soprano approach to negotiating throws the old rule book out the window. He doesn't care much for the carefully articulated phases of negotiation, doesn't prepare with memos putting forward his proposal, doesn't always state his position, debate or discuss, doesn't endure rounds of unnecessary quid pro quo bargaining. He has only one thing in mind: his ideal outcome and how to get there fast.

On *The Sopranos,* negotiation can hurt. If intimidation or violence is a faster path to agreement, then that's okay with Tony and company. It comes as no surprise when Christopher says, "This ain't negotiation time. This is *Scarface,* final scene, fuckin' bazookas under each arm, 'say hello to my little friend.'" The more nefarious the line of business, the more likely Tony and his crew are to use strong-arm tactics. But most of the time he negotiates without resorting to threats.

Tony makes negotiations personal, either negotiating with people he knows or getting to know the people he's negotiating with. He makes negotiations fast. He remains flexible, aware that there are many ways to win. And he's not afraid to squeeze, or stand his ground. The Newark esplanade project, for example, results in a slew of thorny negotiations for Tony, none more important than those with Carmine and his slippery underboss Johnny Sack. It's a negotiation with a powerful mob family and a lot is at stake. Even so, Tony stands firm. By acting as if he is willing to walk away, he effectively gives himself the upper hand. When Sack asks Tony what it would take to reach an accord, Tony has details and numbers. The result? Compromises are made, and Tony walks away with an agreement that guarantees both peace and profit.

Less Is More

What is the best way to avoid lengthy, drawn out negotiations? Avoid them. When Tony negotiates from a position of power, with Uncle Junior, one of his captains or a weak business partner, he doesn't discuss or haggle. He states his terms and that's that.

In corporate America and beyond, many managers and legal departments are embracing the "less is more" philosophy. When one party has all the power, they use a standard contract and accept few changes. Many city and state governments, for example, use boilerplate contracts that vendors are obliged to sign without negotiation or discussion. A different version of the "less is more" approach occurs when companies are courting, such as when a corporation is hiring a consulting firm. The managers at the consulting firms tend to be clear about costs. If the client isn't willing to play (and pay), then they don't waste any more time; they don't wait until the contract phase to learn that they have ir-reconcilable differences.

Say No

Practice saying no, and you will become a better negotiator. As a buyer, when you say no it proves that you mean business. As a seller it shows that you understand the value of the product or service for sale and you're not simply going to accept the highest offer. As Harvey Mackay notes, "No one ever went broke because he said no too often."[1] If selling is about convincing people there's something they can't live without, then negotiating is about telling them you can.

Whether he's the buyer or the seller, Tony is pretty good at saying no. Take for example, a sticky moment during a negotiation with An-nalisa Vittorio, the sexy successor to the throne of the Italian mob fam-ily. Even at his most charming and polite (he's in the old country, after all), what does Tony say to her when she pushes for too low a price on stolen cars? "Up your ass."

It's Personal

Whether Tony is negotiating with his sister Janice or the head of a con-struction company, he makes it personal. When he doesn't know the person sitting across from him at the table, he gets to know him. Nego-tiations, after all, are about people, not dates and dollars. And a negoti-ation starts long before the two parties sit down to hammer out an agreement; a negotiation starts when the parties first meet. So by the time Tony has struck a deal with the charismatic Reverend James, the

African-American activist who is leading protests against the Joint Fitters Union, the two are, if not comrades in arms, then certainly business pals. Tony even gets to know the reverend's father. Because it's personal, Tony has a good sense of the reverend's needs and goals. This helps them both to cut through the crap when they talk, and they are able to hurdle possible obstacles.

Keeping negotiations personal means erecting a bridge of trust between two parties with different needs. Tempers may flare, but trust should not be strained, and when the negotiation turns to enmity, the good negotiator will return to the personal bridge, to trust and shared vision.

There is, of course, an invisible line. Personal does not mean soft, and it doesn't mean showing your hand. Tony's not a pushover, just because he establishes a rapport with the other party in a negotiation. Nor does he show his hand. Effective negotiation is about trust but not wholesale sharing. So Tony is never duplicitous, but nor does he waltz in and announce fears or hidden agendas.

Research

Before you make a business pitch, it's a good idea to find out as much as you can about the company you are pitching. Similarly, before you enter into a negotiation, do your homework: find out about the people who will be signing the agreement and understand the implications of various settlement scenarios. The more you know about the other party and the different possible outcomes, the better you will be able to negotiate. Knowledge is power. Before going to Italy to strike a deal for stolen luxury cars, Tony asks Uncle Junior for the lowdown on the boss of the family with whom he will be negotiating.

Good negotiators make sure they have gathered all the information relevant to the deal. And they make sure the information is correct and up-to-date. Tony gets the poop on the head of the Italian family, only to find out that the man takes no part in the family business any longer. And the research rule applies to both buyer and seller. Before he buys a house on the New Jersey shore, Tony researches the market and brushes up on escrow laws.

Get There Fast

Successful negotiators adhere to a simple rule of thumb: 80 percent of the negotiation is done during or before the first ten minutes. Good negotiators get to the table fast, make sure the right people are present, and then get down to brass tacks. Few people have time to waste anymore on elaborate negotiation tactics, smoke screens, taking pawns instead of queens or the disingenuousness of pushing hard for every little detail.

Watch Tony when called in to meet with Jack Massarone, whose construction project is being hamstrung by the protests against the Joint Fitters Union. Tony arranges a meeting and the first words out of his mouth are "What do you want?" Jack explains the situation, and Tony is equally expeditious in putting his most important card on the table. "It's going to cost you," he says. They can work out details later, but now they have a proposed solution and both parties know that it will be expensive. When and how much can be figured out later. Tony says he'll see what he can do, and the two-minute negotiation is over.

Tony also speeds up negotiations by cutting down on paperwork. He's not exactly a contract guy. While this may not be an option for most of us, there are probably some deals that can be done on a handshake. In most businesses, there are instances where a deal memo will suffice, saving the time and money associated with drafting a formal contract. Alternately, if there is a standing agreement in place, don't renegotiate, just sign an amendment.

Now Slow Down

Tony is not like most of us. His negotiations (when he negotiates at all) are fast. The process is rarely iterative; there are few lawyers involved, little debate and no paper. Try as we might, the rest of us can't always effect such a speedy negotiation.

We can't always be like Tony. Sometimes a negotiation involves more than just an espresso and a handshake. Lawyers do get involved; contracts get printed and revised; time passes. Reaching an agreement is essentially a conversation, a give-and-take iterative process, and many people take a pro forma, process-based approach to negotiating. It's like making pottery: you mold and shape the bowl as the clay spins around the wheel. You give up something; you get something in return. You may have to resort to a little negotiation gamesmanship: ask for something that isn't really important in order to get something in return that you value more. But don't go full tilt on a "need to win" course. It's give-and-take until the shape of the agreement is satisfactory to both parties, or, as lawyers often say, both parties are equally dissatisfied.

Even though Tony doesn't go in for lengthy negotiations, when necessary he slows down and plays by the old rules, as evidenced by his negotiation style with the Italian family buying stolen cars from his import-export subsidiary.

So if you take longer to reach an agreement than the few minutes it takes to drink a cup of coffee or take a stroll in the park, that's okay. None of us wants to take more time than necessary on a contract, but when we need to, we slow down. Remember, that agreement is the law you'll abide by until it is fulfilled or the term expires. Also, it's important to realize that time can be a useful ally in a negotiation. It calms tempperaments, clarifies issues and usually has the effect of clearing the room of people and issues that are unnecessary to the final agreement. So be patient. Five people may show up on the first day of negotiations. A week later, however, some of the original five won't still be there, and it is easier to reach an accord with two people than five.

The Flexible Negotiator

Negotiations rarely work when neither side is willing to give up anything. Good negotiators will concede lesser points to show good faith, earn trust and get themselves in a position to ask for something they consider more important. This means the flexible negotiator is willing to acquiesce on what isn't vital. How do you do that? Figure out in advance what is most important to you and what you can live without. Focus on the big picture, and remember there may be more than one solution to a given problem. Witness Tony negotiating with Uncle Junior. He lets the old man push for rank and title, while quietly holding out for money and power.

When negotiations reach an impasse, flexibility and creativity can save the day. The successful negotiator is able to explore a wide range of options. If you can't get exactly what you want, maybe there's something else you can win instead. Manufacturers will often accept punishing terms on one order, if it comes with the guarantee of another piece of business. Political deputies are adept at reviving negotiations by taking a different tack, approaching the problem from a new direction.

Tony remains flexible at the negotiating table. If the other side pushes hard for one thing, he tries to get something else. So when Reverend James won't come down on the split of moneys being extorted from Massarone to put an end to the Joint Fitters Union protests, Tony looks for a new opportunity. He puts something else on the table, something that may mean more than a lucrative split: "What do you hear about the public school asbestos removal project over in Carney?" Tony asks. And they're on their way to reaching an agreement on another piece of business. Nor does Tony leave it at that. After he and Reverend James have agreed to terms and have identified another lucrative project, Tony brings it back to the personal level. "Sorry about your old man," he says. And soon the two men are chatting about parents, aging, history, family.

Squeeze, or Stand Firm

It's okay to squeeze during a negotiation. Interpretation: it's all right to stand firm. A good leader knows what she wants, has itemized and prioritized her objectives and knows what she's willing to concede before she walks into a negotiation. That way the outcome is never really surprising.

Tony knows what he wants when he negotiates with Johnny Sack. So when Sack demands a 40 percent cut of the Housing and Urban Development scam, Tony says no. He then calls back to counter with a low-ball offer. Both Johnny and Tony keep the negotiation focused and stick to the major points.

Negotiation primers stress the importance of knowing your "Best Alternative to a Negotiated Agreement," or BATNA. To negotiate successfully, you must know what the most attractive alternative is for you. Similarly, if you have a good sense of the other party's BATNA, it will allow you to strengthen or reexamine your terms.

Uncle Junior, not the most skilled negotiator, comes to the bargaining table with verbal diarrhea. When he and Tony sit down to discuss Junior's cut, the old man talks a blue streak. Tony, on the other hand, says little. He's a BATNA man; he knows Uncle Junior's alternatives are limited at best. So Tony listens, nods, then tells Uncle Junior that their split stays the same.

Like any good negotiator, Tony doesn't show his hand at the negotiating table. So when he and Carmela are working out a punishment for Meadow's involvement in trashing her grandmother's house, Tony reminds Carmela that they cannot let it be known that they are negotiating from a position of weakness.

There is one thing you rarely see Tony do while negotiating, and that's lose his temper. It doesn't help to blow your top during a negotiation. It only exposes your weaknesses, undermines the good faith that's been built and slows things down.

Leaders Lead

It is the job of the leader to decide when to negotiate. Most leaders agree that whether negotiations take place quickly or not, there is no need to rush into them.

Just as leaders decide when their team gets involved in a negotiation, they must also decide when and how people are deployed. A negotiation, after all, is just another project. And people and resources must be prudently allocated. For example, if 80 percent of the negotiation is effectively concluded in the first ten minutes, as is often the case, then it makes sense that the time-strapped executive need not sit through every minute of the remainder of the negotiation. Similarly, term sheets at the beginning of a negotiation will save time by getting both parties to agree upon multiple terms that will govern the agreement. Then, it's the job of the leader to get the negotiation on track and to agree in principle on the big issues. Many leaders find they don't need to get bogged down in the back-and-forth, the language and minutiae. They let trusted lawyers, associates or project managers work through the details.

Even if there is no one else who can finish the negotiation, as is the case in many small businesses, get through the big stuff first and table the details for a later date. If you cannot opt out of the negotiation after the big issues have been agreed upon, then maybe the other party can. Finish up with their lawyers, or select an agreement "point person," preferably someone who is not your main client contact, not the person with whom you have the strongest personal relationship. That way, you can develop a trusting relationship with someone else at the organization, and you won't get your main client relationship off track by focusing on a barrage of contract details, rather than sticking to the big-picture issues. Finally, if you find yourself spending days on end poring over contract details, maybe it's time to hire a lawyer or delegate some or all of the negotiation process.

It Never Ends

After the contract is signed, think about how the process could be improved. What lessons did you learn from the other guys? Especially after a long negotiation or in new area of business, make notes on what worked and what didn't work. Then, during the life cycle of the project or client, write down what you overlooked during the negotiation phase or what contractual language might be helpful in the future. Some executives find it helpful to keep a list of these negotiation rules, a document they update after each contract is signed and refer to every time they begin a new negotiation.

Case Study

Anita works for a large real estate company that owns and manages two adjacent buildings on a busy shopping street. A national retailer is interested in renting the entire ground floor of both buildings, but only if they can create a single space—with a new entrance, different orientation and redesigned facade. The real estate company wants the retailer as a tenant, but negotiations get off to a rocky start. The lawyers on

Anita's team are adamant about not moving the entrance or redesigning the facade, actions they believe will anger and possibly push out existing tenants.

After the first day's negotiations lead nowhere, Anita speaks to her boss, who says the company can live with moving the store's entrance, but the retailer cannot have free rein over design. "On the other hand," he says, "we're willing to come down on rent to make them happy. We really want this tenant."

They try again the following day. But there are too many issues, like infrastructure problems, liability insurance, construction time frames. Things are going nowhere fast.

Enter Don, lawyer for the retailer. Anita senses that Don is as frustrated as she is, and she gets the feeling that he's the key decision maker. When Don steps out to take a phone call, Anita excuses herself as well. Standing beside the elevator bank, the two of them hash out an ad hoc agreement. Anita goes straight for the big stuff. They can move the entrance, but Anita's company gets to approve any architectural plans that affect the facade. "If we can get this wrapped up by the end of the week," she promises, "we'll come down five percent on the first year's rent." Don agrees.

When the two reenter the conference room, Don and Anita tell the two teams that they have reached an agreement on big issues. And just like that, they're ordering sandwiches and hashing out details.

Don and Anita took the negotiation out of the confrontational conference room, where both teams had lawyers with lists of potential hurdles. Each, in his or her own way, was direct, flexible and focused on a satisfactory end result. They agreed on the big stuff, then went back to the conference room to iron out details, with the result that they negotiated and signed an important lease in a relatively short period of time.

THE WRAP-UP

Effective negotiation is an essential part of business, and there's no substitute for experience, so the only way to get better at negotiating is to do it, with an eye to learning and improving. Of course, you can and should do your homework before every negotiation: research, rehearse, predict scenarios. The Tony Soprano approach focuses on tactics and techniques aimed at faster, better negotiation.

- If you don't need to negotiate, don't. If a handshake or deal memo will suffice, then skip the lengthy contract.

- Know what you want, what terms you will accept and your best alternative to the agreement before you sit down at the bargaining table.

- Find out about the other people sitting at the table.

- You negotiate with a person, not a company. Allow it to be personal, and modify your approach depending on the personality sitting across from you. If she's a detail hound, then be prepared for the negotiation rumba. If he's a bully, find things to concede that appear to be bigger concessions than they really are.

- Don't rush into a negotiation. And once you're sitting down, don't rush through the agreement.

- Stay focused on your ideal outcome, and how to achieve it with the minimum time and fuss.

- Delegate and save time. If possible, agree on important terms quickly, then hand over the details to someone else.

- Be flexible. If there's an impasse, try to find creative alternatives.

- Review. After a negotiation, think about what went well and what could have gone better.

- Make rules. Write down a list of rules and reminders so that it goes better next time.

■ **WORKSHEET** ■
Prepare to Negotiate

Lack of preparedness, conviction, knowledge or tact can hinder a negotiation. Be prepared for every negotiation.

Who are you negotiating with? Who are the decision makers? What are their real goals and needs?

_____

_____

Do your homework about the person you will be negotiating with. How can you get to know him better?

_____

_____

Is he going to take a long time or go straight for the dealbreakers?

_____

_____

Who is on your team? How will they make the greatest contribution?

_____

_____

What are your main objectives? What are your limits? The highest price? Shortest turnaround time?

_____

_____

What is your Best Alternative to a Negotiated Agreement (BATNA)? What is the BATNA of the person you'll be negotiating with? (If your BATNA is more attractive than the current offer, then don't accept the offer.)

_____

_____

Think laterally: how can you change the terms and still make both parties happy?

_____

_____

Are you spending too much time poring over contracts? Who else in your organization could lead some or all negotiations?

_____

_____

Still too stressed out? Do you need the help of a lawyer, associate, union or business organization?

_____

_____

Think about your most recent negotiation. What could you have done better? What did you learn from the other party involved?

_____

_____

TWELVE

WHAT CARMELA KNOWS: MANAGING UP

Up, Down and Sideways Management

When Tony has a problem, Carmela has a problem. Like when Tony's sister Janice tries to borrow money using their mother's house as collateral and Tony blows his lid, it's up to Carmela to keep the peace. "Why don't you grow the fuck up," she snaps, and Tony calms down.

Carmela is managing up. It may be risky, but it's important. Tony is unpredictable, quick to anger, and slow to forgive. Yet Carmela manages to influence his decisions and modify his behavior. How she does it is testament to the fact that even the biggest boulder can be budged, even the toughest boss can be influenced. It just takes many of the hallmark strategies of the Tony Soprano approach, plus a little extra skill, insight and timing.

Everyone has a boss. Even if you're the big cheese, your client, board of directors, wife or husband is your boss, at least some of the time. And you need to manage up, at least some of the time. Managing up requires consummate skill, combines subtlety with directness, flexibility with impeccable timing. It's not easy to learn, and you don't get a lot of second chances. Fortunately, Carmela is a queen of managing up. And Tony, Livia and others are pretty good at it too.

It's the Same but Different

In many ways, the Carmela Soprano approach to managing up is no different from the Tony Soprano approach to managing in any other direction. It's both fast and flexible. It's about time; specifically it aims to save time, for your boss or those above you, for yourself or for a particular goal or project. And to get it right, you have to remain flexible. When Carmela pays a visit to her neighbor's sister to ask her to write Meadow a letter of recommendation for Georgetown University, she enters the office, is polite, delivers a ricotta pie and her request, then takes her leave, saying that her mother is waiting in the car downstairs. She's in, she's out. Stick and move.

Managing up means saying less to achieve more. When you're dealing with a subordinate, you have the choice between direct ball busting or indirect prodding. When you're managing up, you start with subtlety. You hint, you don't harangue. Even Janice is good at striking quickly, and she knows how to suggest, imply and direct attention in order to manage up. She manipulates Richie, stoking his anger, hinting at the fact that he needs to make a move against Tony. She doesn't come out and say anything specific. Instead she quotes Sun Tzu to her malcontent lover: "When your opponent gives you an opening, be swift as a hare."

The Carmela Soprano approach to managing up favors a highly personal orientation, based on strong individual relationships, trust and understanding. You stand by and love team members, whether they sit in the big office or you do. What does Agent Grasso suggest to Pussy when he needs to ingratiate himself to Tony and avoid suspicion? "Make him love you." And whomever you are managing or influencing, it pays to remember that love and trust go a lot further than bullying and fear. Everyone likes praise, even bosses, even husbands.

At the same time, managing up is an entirely different ball of mozzarella than managing down or sideways. If you treat your boss as if she's your subordinate, you probably won't get very far. Managing up is as reactive as it is proactive, works better in private than public, requires an unusual blend of subtlety and direct communication, badgering and knowing when to stop. Perhaps most important, managing up succeeds only when used judiciously and appropriately: pick your battles and choose the right time.

Carmela's Recipe for Managing Up

Tony is pretty good at it, but when it comes to managing up, Carm is the queen. She picks her battles; her timing is impeccable; she's tactful yet direct. Although the recipe may change slightly depending on the situation, the five main ingredients, or phases, remain basically the same:

- Research

- Agenda

- Outline

- Deploy

- Feedback

Research

Research is vital to any business or managerial venture—and probably the most important part of upward managing. Before you can effect change, you need to research three things.

- *The idea:* Is your idea or program worthwhile? Will it make an appreciable difference to your company, you, your boss?

- *Me:* Am I the right person for this particular project?

- *Them:* Is your boss—or whomever you want to approach—the right person to okay or implement the idea?

THE IDEA

Vision is everything, and you must know why an idea or proposal is important to your vision. It must be worth the trouble. Every time Carmela manages up, the goal is worthwhile—financial security, getting Meadow into a good college, a happier husband.

Managing up is an investment of time, resources and relationship capital. So think about the return-on-investment. Some things aren't worth the hassle. As Carmela knows from her experience with Janice's holiday dinner: Don't cook in someone else's kitchen. You'll only end up doing her dirty dishes.

ME

Before you can manage up, you must understand your needs as well as elements of your style that may impact the implementation of your idea. Take into account your personality type, likes and dislikes. Do you tend to be assertive or indirect? What type of behavior will carry the day? How do you tend to deal with authority figures? Do you need to alter the way you behave in light of those tendencies?

When A.J. gets sent home from school for vandalizing the school swimming pool, the principal is surprisingly lenient on the youth. But Carmela doesn't want valuable life lessons to go unlearned. She knows what she needs and has clearly assessed the costs and benefits of involving Tony. While she realizes it may be tough to get him involved, Carmela also knows that what's at stake is her son's moral fiber, and there's nothing more important to her than her children.

THEM

Once you know why you are managing up and how you might get in your own way, you're ready to move on to making sure you know the person you wish to influence—and formulating a plan.

Managing up is like negotiating. It's important to research—and know—the person you're dealing with. Before you knock on the someone's door, you must understand the person you're trying to influence. Know her goals and objectives, stated or unstated. Understand her strengths and weaknesses, blind spots, obsessions. Learn her prejudices and pet peeves, what pisses her off, the pressures she feels, what she likes. Once you've mastered all of that, then you can approach her.

You must also evaluate your relationship with the person to make sure it's appropriate that you—and not someone else—take action. Just as you should think twice before delegating a task to someone outside your group, you must consider whether it's appropriate that you engage with this person. Carmela has a bone to pick with Livia, but Livia is Tony's mother, so Carmela waits until Tony has tried and failed to control his mother's wrath and manipulation. And when Carm steps in, she is swift and clear and makes it known that she's acting on behalf of Tony. "You know, Ma, your son loves you very much," she says. "I want you to cut the drama. It's killing Tony."

When managing—or selling—up, it is important to tie your proposal to issues of particular interest to the person you're trying to persuade. In Carmela's case, she makes sure Tony knows that she is concerned with Meadow going to college, A.J.'s character development or the family finances. She knows that Tony cares.

Most people don't like being told what to do, especially when it comes from a surprising source. So once you've figured out who you are dealing with, you should nudge him to consider something, to look at a problem. Don't suggest the solution, just focus his attention on the issue you want resolved, remind him about that discussion or problem, then hang back. Carmela works to get Tony to be part of a unified front in dealing with Meadow when their daughter wants to take a year off from college and go to Europe. Carmela knows Tony, knows that he loves his daughter but has a short fuse. So she doesn't tell him what to do, not initially anyway. Rather she focuses her efforts on suggesting that Meadow see a therapist. "We could use an ally here, Tony," she says, and soon enough he's on board.

Of course, no two people are the same. Managing up, down or sideways is personal. Some people won't respond to nudging and hints. The Carmela Soprano approach to managing up allows directness. After subtlety, after getting your issue on the boss's agenda, try clarity and specificity. And if you keep hinting but it's like talking to a wall, then be more direct. When Carmela takes a shot at managing up with Livia, she does not beat around the bush.

Agenda

Okay, so your idea is worthwhile. You've thought about your strengths, weaknesses, style, and you've researched the person you wish to manage. Now you need to get your idea on the radar screen, onto her agenda.

During this phase you integrate what you know about yourself and your boss—and focus on your proposal. Carmela integrates what she knows about herself with what she knows to be Tony's weaknesses and sensitivities. After A.J. is sent home for vandalizing the school swimming pool, she persuades Tony that it's a serious matter and requires the attention of both parents. When they confront the boy, they present a unified front in doling out strict discipline, including a tougher curfew.

You've heard it before: it's the relationship, stupid. Managing up is not a one-time thing, it's all about developing an appropriate relationship for effecting change. That relationship must suit both of your needs and personality types, and it must be built on mutual trust and respect. You can't nag or argue all day every day, and you can't expect to monopolize your boss's time or resources. Rather you must focus his attention, keep him informed, help him to see a problem the way you see it and arrive at the same conclusion.

Of course, your boss is busy. That's why getting your idea on her agenda is probably the trickiest part of managing up. It requires tact and sensitivity. "Hey, we should talk about staff bonuses some time," is a good way to suggest a topic without appearing to bully or show your hand. Try not to nag, but you may have to do so, to remind her to get the conversation started.

FINESSE FIRST

Even Uncle T manages up from time to time. And when he does, he's adroit. Observe Tony after a grand jury has been empaneled to investigate mob activities. He doesn't interrupt Uncle Junior, doesn't contradict, doesn't say much of anything. Even when asked directly, he doesn't demur. Rather he goes out of his way to agree with his uncle. Quietly, a few minutes later, he does add the simple suggestion that they should be careful, destroy evidence, cover their tracks. This allows Uncle Junior to agree, without the appearance of contradiction. Tony gets what he wants. Uncle Junior doesn't feel challenged or undermined. Everyone's happy.

As brash as he can be, Tony persuades rather than instructs. When he manages subordinates, Tony coaches, and when he deals with partners, he suggests. Only when that fails does he resort to bullying and demands. Subtlety and finesse are the hallmarks of the first salvo of any upward management. Don't lay it all on the line the first time you mention something to your boss. It's okay to hint, to be subtle, even vague. How does Livia suggest to Junior that he should go after Tony? "Don't let certain people take advantage of your good nature." Enough said.

BE DIRECT

Once you have gotten your issue on the boss's radar screen, then you can be more direct. When Carmela is trying to talk to Tony about something, she employs a soft approach first, then she pushes a bit harder. Contrary to the accepted wisdom about managing up, Carmela's approach allows for a certain amount of pushing and prodding. It's okay to squeeze. For example, when Carmela wants to discuss the family's financial situation and put money into stocks and mutual funds, she badgers Tony until he agrees to talk to her—and an expert.

You may start the process by nudging, but eventually managing up requires good, direct communication. It pays to get to the point fast, then be succinct and polite. So when she meets with Jean Cusamano's sister, Carmela is courteous and quick, but also firm: "I don't think you understand," she says with a smile. "I want you to write that letter."

Directness is good, even when things are bad. Be honest about what's wrong. If you're trying to change something, explain your idea specifically. When he's sulking and morose, Tony gets an earful of directness, Carmela-style: "You're like an alien life form among us."

Outline

When it all starts to come together, when you have your boss's attention, you need to outline your idea. First, provide a summary or a simple proposal. Then, you may need to provide specifics on how to implement. Like managing any project, you want to articulate strategy and broad strokes first. Save the specifics of the action plan for later. And try not to micromanage. When Carmela wants Tony to make a hefty donation to Columbia University, she outlines the idea and the benefits—what she wants to donate and the recognition they'll receive as donors.

Because you are not the boss when you're managing up, you should be putting topics on the table, rather than showing up with slides and spreadsheets, tactical plans or budgets. Sure, you should have a specific plan detailing where you want to go and how to get there, but, like Carmela, you want to outline your approach and let the boss or coworkers have some input.

Once the issue is being discussed, you bring out the spreadsheets. In a recent study, more than two-thirds of managers said they use the logic of a business plan to sell an issue to senior management. Proposals for change are most favorably received when they are supported by specific numbers and forecasts, charts, facts, and action plans.[1]

Deploy

You know yourself. You know them. They've signed on. Okay, time to get to work. This is the action phase: integrate and activate. Incorporate your research and planning—what you know about yourself with what you know about the person you're seeking to influence—to develop a method of managing up that meets your needs and suits his temperament. You want to be part of the implementation team, not someone pretending to be boss for a day.

Deployment may mean doing the project you've instigated, or it may mean pitching in. After Carmela gets Tony to agree to talk to a financial consultant, she sets up the meeting and arrives prepared with notes and questions for the expert. Deployment may also be a matter of sitting back and waiting, as with Carmela's prodding Tony to make a contribution to Meadow's college.

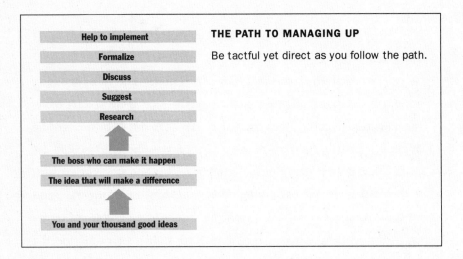

Feedback

You've done it. Your big idea has seen the light of day. Now make sure you gather feedback. Review the project, try to measure its success and get a sense of people's opinions, not only that of your boss but the thoughts of others impacted by the plan you implemented. Check opinions and measurements against your original vision or strategy.

Case Study

An art gallery has fallen on hard times. The downturn in the economy has resulted in a slackening in art sales, while their rent has remained constant and other budget items have not decreased. Karl, the manager, responsible for day-to-day operations of the gallery, realizes there are fiscal problems when he calls a freelance installer for an upcoming show only to hear that the installer hasn't been paid in months. Later, he learns that his boss, Susan, has made appointments with her accountant and a loan officer at their bank.

Karl is worried. He knows that things like budgets and fiscal planning are not his responsibility. But he's concerned that if he doesn't make them his responsibility, then the gallery might go out of business or he might lose his job. He starts to make a list of ways the gallery could cut costs. They could stop paying for a storage facility and store the artwork in their basement and back room. They could buy used computers and office furniture. They could stop hiring a freelance designer to create every postcard announcing every show. Karl could do it, or Maggie, the gallery registrar, could take over some design work. It would increase their workload, sure, but isn't that better than losing their jobs?

The problem is that Susan, the boss, doesn't ask for suggestions. Nor is she very forthcoming about the specifics of their financial woes or the exact steps she is taking. Karl considers his needs and goals and thinks through Susan's position before taking the first step. And then he suggests to her that they talk about budget issues sometime. Susan nods but doesn't act on his suggestion. So he tries again. "Hey, by the way, we still gotta have that chat about budget stuff," he says when they're locking up one evening. Sure enough, she agrees to have a quick meeting.

When they meet, Karl doesn't launch into his suggestions, doesn't pull out his spreadsheets. He listens, lets Susan rail against the economy and young collectors, and asks her questions. He lets some time pass, and then he makes some suggestions. Susan meets with him once, then again, and they discuss his concerns. Nor is Karl all diffidence and subtlety. When Susan tells him that something can wait awhile, Karl says no it can't and explains why. The next time they sit down, he has budgets in hand, and they streamline the freelancer file, make a schedule for moving out of the storage space, agree on tasks that Karl and Maggie might be able to accomplish. A month later, it is Karl who accompanies Susan to the bank where they get a small business loan.

Desperately Seeking Initiative

Don't be afraid of managing up, just because it's difficult. And if you're the boss, don't resent people trying to manage up; don't close yourself off from new ideas. Poor leaders shy away from situations where something is being asked of them. They don't listen to subordinates, don't take advice. Good leaders embrace initiative in any form. Which means they're open to the possibility of subordinates expressing their views, articulating new ideas, managing up. They encourage openness, honesty and innovation. They are never too busy to listen to a good idea.

THE WRAP-UP

Carmela would agree that managing up is risky business. It requires skill and patience, tact and flexibility. Know the recipe and get it right:

- Pick your battles and choose the right time to manage up.

- Know the idea: make sure it is worthwhile.

- Know yourself: figure out your own goals and needs.

- Know the person you want to manage: understand his position, his fears and issues.

- Integrate: use that knowledge to manage up effectively.

- Nudge before you push; hint before you hammer.

- It's okay to squeeze; it's okay to nag.

- The more direct you need to be, the more private the setting should be.

- Be quick and nimble: get in, get out, move on.

- Involve your peers, not just your boss, and be a team player rather than trying to be boss for a day.

- Help to implement.

- Evaluate: measure success and poll opinions.

- If you're the boss, be open to people's ideas. Listen to those who try to manage up.

■ WORKSHEET ■
Checklist for Managing Up

So, you think you have good cause to manage up. Before you knock on your boss's door, go through this checklist.

Who are you trying to influence? Have you done your research on her? Are you the right person to approach her about the issue that concerns you?

_____

_____

When is he easy to approach? When is not a good time?

_____

_____

Is your suggestion, idea or complaint something that is likely to arise elsewhere? Is someone else likely to pursue it? Are you getting involved in someone else's affairs for no good reason?

_____

_____

What result do you hope to achieve by managing up? Is it worth the time and effort?

_____

_____

What's the worst that can happen if you fail to make your case persuasively?

_____

_____

What is the best-case scenario if you successfully exert influence?

_____

_____

Is it still worth it?

_____

_____

In ten words or less, write down what you will say to your boss to introduce the topic you want to discuss.

_____

_____

In ten bullet points or less, write down your suggestion or plan. (Don't bring this with you, just make sure it's clear in your mind).

_____

_____

On a single page, type a memo that summarizes the suggestion or plan. (But don't give it to your boss until she asks).

_____

_____

How will you measure success or failure?

_____

_____

Who are the chief participants and beneficiaries? How will you measure their opinions?

_____

_____

THIRTEEN

SINS OF OMISSION: WHAT TONY SOPRANO DOES WRONG

Don't Throw Away This Book

Tony Soprano is not an ideal leader, boss, husband or father. What does he do wrong? Lots of stuff. For starters, he's unfaithful and he's killed people. And continues to kill people. And he lies, mainly about being unfaithful and killing people. He says it comes with the territory, that he's a soldier fighting a war. Maybe so, but his sins and shortcomings—in addition to being criminal much of the time—are liabilities to himself, his family, his team and his company. We all make mistakes, but when a leader falters, the ripples of his mistakes can often be felt throughout the organization. And, unfortunately, when a leader messes up outside the office, it can have detrimental ramifications inside the office. And Tony doesn't do anything half-assed. His crimes and shortcomings are big, glaring, ugly. There are easy lessons to be learned from his errors as a man: They're criminal acts and should be avoided if you want to stay out of jail. There are also lasting lessons to be learned from his errors as a leader.

What Tony Soprano, CEO, Does Wrong

As a manager, Tony makes lots of mistakes. As a leader, he is a work in progress. He usually knows when he has gone down the wrong path, acted too rashly or angrily. Some of his pitfalls are sins of omission, abilities he hasn't mastered, uncompensated personality flaws, unmitigated character lapses.

Chief among Tony's flaws as a leader is his anger and lack of self-knowledge. He is too fast to anger, too quick to bully. When the local Chinese restaurant delivers the wrong food, Tony yells and screams, "Motherfucking goddamn orange peel beef." Not your typical person responding to a typical mistake. He knows he has a short fuse, nonetheless his anger continues to define his life. Violent outbursts trip him up constantly and are the subject of many therapy sessions. What happens when Ralph sets fire to a stable? Ask Luca Brazzi. When Tony's lawyer hears that the feds are after him in connection with the homicide of Matt Bevilaqua, he advises his client to "keep cool and don't give them anything." Good advice, but cool ain't exactly Tony's strong suit.

Tony doesn't know himself, not really. Despite his soul searching and Dr. Melfi's intervention, he hasn't conquered his anger, panic attacks or depression. Sure, he's on his way. He knows enough to explain to A.J. after he snaps at him, "I said it because of all the anger and frustration. . . . The last few days it built up inside me and exploded." Nonetheless, his anger continues to build up and explode, and at times Tony can neither understand nor control it. Effective leaders know themselves and maintain an even keel, at least at the office.

Another of Tony's managerial shortcomings is his selfishness. He puts himself before anyone else, doesn't empathize or think through how his actions will impact others, seems to care more about animals than people. Leadership is about other people. Bob Haas, Chairman of Levi Strauss, believes that there are two essentials required of good leaders: "The first is the value of people; the second is the importance of values."[1]

Tony is not the best listener. He interrupts people, doesn't hear explanations, doesn't listen to people's problems or invite others to voice concerns. He says "shut up" a lot and walks away in the middle of conversations. He mocks Silvio when he tries to talk about how he feels and turns a deaf ear to Carmela's confessions of anxiety or distress. When leaders don't listen, they effectively ignore significant information and build resentment. Tony doesn't listen to Paulie, doesn't honor his ambitions or make him feel like he has sufficient potential in the business, and the result is that Paulie talks to Johnny Sack and the New York family.

Tony is not the best communicator. Granted, he is concise and clear when he communicates. But too often he fails to communicate, loses his temper or fails to make himself understood. He bullies and shouts when he should talk and explain. Nor is he good at expressing praise or sympathy. "Get the fuck back in your fucking office, now," he yells at Davey Scatino, the hapless gambler whose business has been pillaged by Tony and company. Not the best interoffice communication, and not the ideal way to express praise. Leadership is about communication, and good leaders know how to listen, talk and ensure that messages have been communicated.

Tony is prejudiced. He attributes this to his family instinct, his old school philosophy of keeping everything within the Italian-American community. But the truth is, he prejudges and it clouds his decisions. When Meadow brings home an African-American boyfriend from Columbia University, Tony uses derogatory terms like *distoon* and *mulignan* and tells him to stay away from his daughter. Prejudging people or companies, whatever the criteria for that judgment, is unfair to them and detrimental to the leader or business that acts out of bias rather than knowledge.

Tony lies. Granted, he lies more to his wife than to his coworkers. Even so, it forces them to be complicit in his dishonesty—and sets a poor example.

And he intimidates. A lot. It's okay to be tough, to squeeze and push for the good of the organization. But Tony sometimes takes it too far, intimidating friends, family and coworkers instead of taking the time and treating them with respect.

Finally, Tony leads in fits and starts. He promises A.J. he'll be at the last swim meet of the season. After A.J. finishes his big race, he rushes over to the bleachers, but Tony isn't there. Dads can't fail to show up if they promise they'll be somewhere. And leaders can't lead part-time. Sure, Tony's a good leader—loyal, caring, focused—when he's leading. The problem is he's not always leading. And leadership isn't something you do when you feel like it. Good leaders are at it 24/7—all day, every day. When Tony feels depressed, he's not enthusiastic (enough). When he's in a bad mood, he doesn't communicate (enough). He doesn't always praise (enough) or express his love (enough). Too little or too late is not the stuff of effective leadership.

We All Make Mistakes

We all make mistakes, even leaders, even good leaders. What separates the ones who will stagnate from those who will grow is the ability to learn from mistakes. Poor leaders don't listen to criticism and don't admit their mistakes. They think it will diminish them. Besides, there's always someone else to blame. Good leaders, on the other hand, know they are fallible. They find the truth in any criticism and look at why things go wrong. They examine their behaviors and search for errors in strategy, delegation or communication. Could they have focused on a more important project? Could they have delegated a task to someone more likely to succeed? Explained something better? That's not to say good leadership is about taking responsibility for other people's errors. But we need to assess what we might have done better, acknowledge our own mistakes and then learn from them.

Annalisa Vittorio tells Tony that he is his own worst enemy. And he's pretty sure she's right. He says to Dr. Melfi, "I bring all of this on myself." So he is becoming aware of his faults; he is moving toward self-knowledge. More than that, he's trying to fight back, to compensate for weaknesses, to try harder, to do better. Leaders are learners, and Tony learns from his mistakes. Also, leaders learn from the faults of others, and we can all learn from Tony's lapses and shortcomings even as we study his many leadership strengths.

LEARN FROM ERRORS

Leaders must review projects and monitor progress, always look-ing at what went wrong or what could be better next time:

➤ Make lists of errors made and lessons learned.

➤ Figure out what caused errors and what worked to fix them.

➤ Don't look to blame someone. Look to figure out why and avoid it happening again.

➤ Ask delegates and subordinates to think about how things could be improved.

Ripples of Wrong

Leaders set the tenor of their organizations. And lapses, omissions and screwups can do significant damage. All eyes are on our leaders, whether they know it or not, and so their slipups have ripples far be-yond their immediate consequences. The ripples can include the ero-sion of morale or the straining of loyalties, and the wounds can take a lot of time to heal.

You must work on your faults and omissions. But first you need to be aware of them—and their consequences. Take the Bevilaqua murder. Tony finds the schmuck who put a bullet in Christopher, drives out to where the youth is hiding out, then shoots him in the heart. Tony may have his reasons for doing the hit himself, but it is something he should delegate. And doing something he should delegate, missing other important engagements, failing to communicate, getting himself in police and federal agent spotlights—all these things send shock waves through the organization. He effectively throws the entire company, not to mention his family, against the wall. With one bullet, he puts on the brakes and disrupts everything.

When they screw up, leaders halt processes and jam the machinery of business. Leaders' slips and faults open doors to a myriad of problems large and small. Tony's capriciousness and anger drive Paulie to talk to the enemy. Leaders' flaws set bad examples and make paltry role models. Look at the impressionable Christopher. He watches Tony; he acts like him. So it comes as no surprise when he shoots a shop clerk in the foot for no good reason. Christopher took in violence with mother's milk, and he's seen Tony's explosions of rage ever since coming to work for him.

Leadership Poster Boy?

While he has a natural talent for leadership and many of the skills of a new breed of manager, Tony doesn't always get it right. And one of these days he might wind up dead. But that doesn't mean his approach is not valuable or well suited for today's business environment. He may not always get it right. Of course, getting it right is pretty tough when you're managing angry, gun-toting sociopaths engaged in dangerous, illegal businesses. And Tony is aware of his faults—and working on them. So he may become a better leader. In the meantime, we should learn his

■ **WORKSHEET** ■
Managerial Traps and Pitfalls

We all have potential pitfalls, and if we know them, know how to spot them before they become problems, then we can be more effective, levelheaded leaders. What are your leadership blind spots? What areas are you working to improve?

What are your managerial weaknesses or blind spots? How are you working to improve as a leader?

_____

_____

_____

What was the last mistake you made? How did you learn from the experience?

_____

_____

_____

Do you lose your temper? Often? When? Is it sometimes unjustified? Is your anger out of proportion to the stimulus?

_____

_____

_____

Are you a good listener? Do you take the time to talk to people about their goals and problems? Do you listen carefully, empathetically?

_____

_____

_____

Do you communicate well? Do you make sure your message has been received and understood? Do you make sure each team member understands her role and goals?

_____

_____

_____

When something goes wrong, do you look for someone else to blame? Who is the last person you blamed for a mistake? Was some of the fault yours?

_____

_____

_____

Are you unfair? Do you treat different people differently? Prejudge?

_____

_____

_____

Do you stay focused and enthusiastic? Or does your concentration and enthusiasm appear to wax and wane?

_____

_____

_____

Do you delegate well? Give people responsibility and a sense of ownership?

_____

_____

_____

Does everyone like you, like working with or for you? If not, why not?

_____

_____

_____

What processes do you have in place to ensure that projects are handled successfully? To check progress? To measure goals?

_____

_____

_____

Do you listen to others when they point out your errors or voice complaints?

_____

_____

_____

Are you leading all the time or only when you feel like it or feel up to it?

_____

_____

_____

Are you a good role model all the time?

_____

_____

_____

What errors or shortcomings do you have in common with Tony Soprano as a leader? What are you doing to mitigate and learn from them?

_____

_____

_____

Is there an aspect of leading or managing that you've improved upon? What weaknesses or faults are you currently working on fixing?

_____

_____

_____

strategies, not copy all of his tactics; focus on his business methods not his business ideas. We should take away what Tony does well and learn from his shortcomings, even as we try to learn from our own.

THE WRAP-UP

Hey, no one said it was gonna be easy. Being a leader is difficult; the path strewn with pitfalls and problems. Even if you don't have murder and infidelity on your managerial rap sheet, you probably aren't perfect. Chances are your faults are different from Tony's. Maybe you don't delegate enough. Maybe you're too diffident. Maybe you have your favorite people and projects. Do you communicate too infrequently? Do you make things too complicated? Expect too much? Too little? Whenever there's a problem, whenever you feel angry or inadequate or battered down by a bad day at the office, ask yourself why and what went wrong. Then try to fix it.

Knowing yourself means knowing your weaknesses. Being the best leader you can be means admitting when you screw up and knowing that you can learn from your mistakes. Being the best means learning from failure, minimizing imperfections and maximizing strengths. Being the best you can be means working at being an even better leader, twenty-four hours a day, in the office and after work. And it means working on weaknesses, faults, sins of omission, so that they're less of a problem and eventually not a problem at all. George Santayana said, "Those who do not learn the lessons of history are doomed to repeat them." It's the same with leadership. Those who forget the lessons of leadership, those who don't learn from their own mistakes or the mistakes of others, are doomed to repeat them.

HERE COMES TONY

The Right Stuff

Tony Soprano is an effective leader, because each facet of his leadership style responds to the needs of his business, meets the challenges served up by competitors and reflects how his people work. Because his business environment is in constant motion, Tony is fast, flexible and direct. Because his company is arrayed over diverse areas and relies on complex partnerships, he is decisive and quick to implement changes. Because his business is all about people, he puts stock in trust, respect and responsibility, and knows how to delegate. Because his industry is a difficult one and times are tough, he has a clear vision of his life and work, and he squeezes subordinates and business partners to make good on that vision. Because he wants his team to succeed, he instills trust and loves his people. When there are deals to be made, he negotiates quickly and well. When conflicts arise, he resolves them.

The Tony Soprano approach is ideally suited to today's global business and economic environment. In an age of corporate decline, jittery financial markets and wary consumers, proactive, honest, powerful leaders may be the key to restoring confidence and rebuilding balance sheets. We need leaders with a transparent, direct style. We need innovators and change managers. We need leaders we trust, leaders who are good role models, effective communicators and coaches, leaders with a passion to lead, who are not afraid to squeeze and have the drive to succeed.

Take-Aways

Taking the Tony Soprano approach may mean that you work faster, delegate more or squeeze harder. Perhaps it means that you keep an eye out for innovation and an ear open to suggestion and criticism. Hopefully it will help you to build better teams, avoid and resolve conflict, manage up, know yourself and negotiate better. It definitely means that you think about your vision for yourself and your organization and that you become a leader or player who is trustworthy, transparent and flexible. But it does not mean that you show up to work tomorrow and slam someone against the filing cabinets. Sorry, you can't attack 'em, and you still can't whack 'em.

There's Two Endings

Tony knows the dangers associated with his profession and rank. He knows that neither paranoia nor precautions can guarantee his safety. As he explains to Dr. Melfi, "There's two endings for a guy like me—dead or in the can." That he has survived as long as he has—and succeeded as well as he has—is a testament to his leadership ability. And you get the feeling that his downfall, if and when that happens, will not be the result of leadership lapses, but the fatal endgame of luck, timing or hubris.

For the rest of us, if we do what Tony does well without the fits of rage, depression and plots, then we can use the Tony Soprano approach to be more successful leaders and live happier, more fulfilled lives.

The Tony Soprano Approach: Take Home a Box

It's new, it's old, it's straightforward, it's unorthodox. It works. The Tony Soprano approach is a leadership paradigm that responds to shifts in the world in which we work, maps to the organizations we work for and suits the way we live. And don't look now, but Tony Soprano leaders are beginning to appear around the world, in both the public and private sector.

And they're just in time. Recent polls show that 46 percent of Americans believe every company is involved in wrongdoing in one way or another.[1] Meanwhile, corporate scandals continue, downsizing is the norm, public trust has frayed, governance has eroded, ethics have been trampled, and many of yesteryear's corporate giants have shrunk or died. In 2000, 20 percent of Fortune 500 CEOs were fired or forced to resign.[2] And a 2002 poll found that three in four Americans believe top executives take improper actions.[3]

Do we like and trust our business leaders? Fuggedaboudit. Do we need vision and innovation and leaders who can get us there? We sure do. Are we ready for the new-style old school, the directness, transparency, vision and respect of the Tony Soprano approach? You better believe it. Cue music: "Born under a bad sign, you got the blue moon in your eyes."[4] Wait for it . . . A car drives across a bridge, an elevator bell rings, office doors open. From factories to board rooms, from mob offices to management suites, in overalls and pin-striped suits, as morning coffees are sipped and newspapers scanned, a golden age of leadership is dawning. Here comes Tony.

THE RULES

Uncle T believes in rules. He doesn't run around spouting favorite maxims, but he lives by a code and expects others to do the same. Here are some of the rules that encapsulate the Tony Soprano approach:

- You Can't Just Whack 'Em
- Create and Save Time
- Know Yourself
- It's Okay to Squeeze
- Use Your Time Wisely
- Be Direct
- Develop and Share Your Vision for Life and Work
- Make It Personal
- Seek Advice from Experts
- Innovate Now
- Share the Vision
- Be Fair and Consistent
- Be Empathetic
- Learn from the Best
- Listen and Communicate Well
- Build the Right Team
- Love Your Team
- Seek and Deserve Loyalty
- Take Time to Lead
- Be Observant
- Delegate Well
- You Gotta Bust Some Balls
- Be Thoughtful and Generous
- Use Meetings Effectively
- Be Decisive
- Expect Excellence
- Do Unto Others as You Would Have Them Do Unto You
- Use Brains Not Brawn
- Praise in Public; Squeeze in Private
- Apologize When You Screw Up
- Be Fair and Consistent
- Prepare for Negotiations
- Pick Your Battles
- Learn from Your Errors

THE WISDOM OF TONY SOPRANO

Put the wisdom of *Tony Soprano on Management* to work for yourself and your organization:

It's Okay to Squeeze

Shit Runs Downhill

You Gotta Bust Some Balls

Be Decisive

Innovate Now

ENDNOTES

Chapter One

1. Warren Bennis, *On Becoming a Leader* (Cambridge, Massachusetts: Perseus Books, 1989), p. 71.
2. *Ibid.*, p. 56.

Chapter Two

1. Tom Peters, *The Circle of Innovation* (New York: Alfred A. Knopf, 1997), p. 77.
2. *Ibid.*, p. 79.
3. D. A. Benton, *How to Act Like a CEO* (New York: McGraw Hill, 2001), p. 99.
4. Jim Collins, *Good to Great: Why Some Companies Make the Leap . . . and Others Don't* (New York, HarperCollins, 2000), p. 20.
5. Kimberly-Clark U.S. Web site (http://www.kimberlyclark.com/aboutus/ceos_paveway.asp).
6. John Simons, "Power 25," *Fortune*, August 11, 2003.

Chapter Three

1. Sam Walton (with John Huey), *Sam Walton: Made in America: My Story* (New York: Bantam Books, 1993), p. 103.
2. "Speaking Out: IBM's Sam Palmisano," *BusinessWeek*, August 25, 2003.
3. Circadian Technologies, Inc., 2003.
4. Gideon Lichfield, "Meet the New Guys," *Wired*, July 2002.

Chapter Four

1. Fred Vogenstein, "The Amazon Way," *Fortune*, May 26, 2003.

2. Robert Berner, "P & G: New and Improved," *BusinessWeek,* July 7, 2003.
3. John Templeman, "The New Mercedes," *BusinessWeek,* August 26, 1996.
4. Amy Kover, "It's Back. But Can the New Napster Survive?," *The New York Times,* August 17, 2003.

Chapter Five

1. Peter Drucker, *The Effective Executive* (New York: HarperBusiness Essentials, 2002), p. 36–37.

Chapter Nine

1. Noshua Watson, "Not Your Average Headhunter," *Fortune,* July 21, 2003.

Chapter Ten

1. Harvey Mackay, *Swim With the Sharks Without Being Eaten Alive* (New York: Fawcett Books, 1996), p. 192.

Chapter Eleven

1. Harvey Mackay, *Swim With the Sharks Without Being Eaten Alive* (New York: Fawcett Books, 1996), p. 94.

Chapter Twelve

1. John Joseph, "Change Leadership: Selling Up," *Wharton Leadership Digest,* October 2001, Volume 6, Number 1.

Chapter Thirteen

1. D. A. Benton, *How to Act Like a CEO* (New York: McGraw Hill, 2001), p. 4.

Conclusion

1. The American Survey, July 2002.
2. Larry Bossidy, Ram Charan and Charles Burck, *Execution: The Discipline of Getting Things Done* (New York: Crown Business, 2002), p. 14.
3. CNN/*USA Today*/Gallup Poll, July 2002.
4. A3, "Woke Up This Morning" (Geffen Records, 1998).

ACKNOWLEDGMENTS

This book would not have been possible without the love and support of Amanda Davis; the energy and wisdom of my agent, Wendy Silbert; the intelligence and care of my editor, Kimberly Lionetti; or the diligence and patience of John Schneider.

Big thanks to my captains and consultants, Jason Bernhard, Dan Goodman, J. D. Dolan, Lisa Hall, Larry Walsh, Sherri Rifkin, Andrea Schulz and Robert Eversz. A fat envelope of thanks to each of you.

I learned so much from interviews and discussions with Donald Keough, Jack Quinn, Rick Powell, Peter Frampton, Bruce Kelley, Juggler-ga, George McGrath, Lauren Marino, Bill Lyddan, Betsey Locke, Susan Barocas, John Marks, Debra Immergut, Yair Rainer and Scott Moyers. Thank you.

I am grateful to the Virginia Center for Creative Arts for providing a peaceful and beautiful place to write. And thanks to Mass Transmit for email marketing wizardry.

For tireless listening, editing, cheerleading, love and encouragement, I thank my family: June, David, Hope, John, Jack, Sophie, Harry, Joanna, Adam, Tracey and Maxwell.

Finally, three cheers and a ricotta pie to HBO, David Chase and the team of *The Sopranos* for making me a Sunday night TV addict and a better manager—two things that don't usually go together.

MORE INFORMATION, SEMINARS AND SPEAKING ENGAGEMENTS

To find out more about executive coaching, seminars, speaking engagements, leadership and pasta, please visit our Web site:

www.tonysopranoonmanagement.com

This book is available for bulk sales. To inquire about pricing for ten or more copies, please send email to:

sales@tonysopranoonmanagement.com

Wanna bust balls or sing praise? Contact Anthony:

anthony@tonysopranoonmanagement.com

Anthony Schneider is a nationally recognized expert on leadership and management. In addition to writing on the subject, he runs seminars and works as a leadership coach. He was the founder and CEO of Web Zeit, a New York–based Internet strategy firm. Web Zeit's global client roster includes Chase Manhattan, Pfizer, GlaxoSmithKline, Deloitte Touche Tohmatsu and HarperCollins.

Prior to founding Web Zeit, Anthony developed Internet marketing campaigns, online games and interactive strategy. He also worked for two of the world's largest advertising agencies, Dentsu and McCann-Erickson.

Anthony is a graduate of the University of Pennsylvania and New York University. His interests include waste management, Newark waterfront real estate and cooking pasta. He lives in New York City.

INDEX

Page numbers in *italic* indicate illustrations; those in **bold** indicate worksheets.